If Going Makes You a Christian, Then Going into the Garage Makes You a Car!

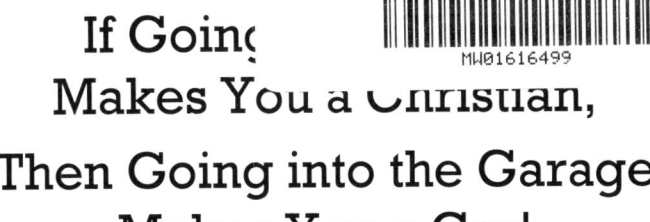

"Whoever abides in Him does not sin. Whoever sins has neither seen Him nor known Him. Little children, let no one deceive you. He who practices righteousness is righteous, just as He is righteous. He who sins is of the devil, for the devil has sinned from the beginning. For this purpose the Son of God was manifested, that He might destroy the works of the devil. Whoever has been born of God does not sin, for His seed remains in him; and he cannot sin, because he has been born of God." 1 John 3:6-9

My Story and Bible Study
A Biblical and Spirit of Prophecy Compilation
To go from professed "Christian"
To Abiding in Christ

Lisa Neuharth
Published 2022

I Give My Thanks and Love To:

God – who has created and pursued me relentlessly for so many years – never giving up – until I finally listened, fell in love, and grew in knowledge. Your love and Your ways truly amaze me! You have completely filled me to overflowing! I am looking forward to today, tomorrow, and eternity together!

My Husband David – for choosing me despite my broken past and unknown future, teaching me love is a principle, and sticking together through thick and thin. I am looking forward to walking through eternity together hand-in-hand.

My Son Lucas – for changing my course in life

My Son Levi – for the passion you bring to this world

My Son Benjamin – for your courage and song

My Mom – for always praying, encouraging, never giving up, always helping, including your tremendous work in editing this book

My Dad – for giving me a love for wisdom, hard work, and perfection

Serenity – for giving me the title to this book and pushing me to answer the hard questions of life

Margarita – for your Holy Spirit inspired art

My Church Family – for true family and friends in Christ - who sing, pray, grow, cry, laugh, call-up, and study the Word together.

No one can serve two masters; for either he will hate the one and love the other, or else he will be loyal to the one and despise the other.
Matthew 6:24

Now may the God of peace Himself sanctify you completely; and may your whole spirit, soul, and body be preserved blameless at the coming of our Lord Jesus Christ. He who calls you is faithful, who also will do it.
1 Thessalonians 5:23-24

Here is the patience of the saints; here are those who keep the commandments of God and the faith of Jesus.
Revelation 14:12

STOP

**Choose
you this day
whom you will serve...
but as for me and my
house, we will serve
the Lord."
Joshua 24:15**

Whoever commits sin is a slave of sin. John 8:34

He who is not with Me is against Me. Matthew 12:30

But your iniquities have separated you from your God: and your sins have hidden His face from you. Isaiah 59:2

"As I live," says the Lord God, "I have no pleasure in the death of the wicked, but that the wicked turn from his way and live. Turn, turn from your evil ways! For why should you die?"
Ezekiel 33:11

3

Abiding in Christ – Introduction

Abiding in Christ - Different Aspects

Before You Read On….

This is a Warning…
Do You Have Faith?
Real Faith?...
Because Truth is Meaningless,
Without Faith.

Hebrews 11:1 Now faith is the substance of things hoped for, the evidence of things not seen.
Hebrews 11:6 Without faith it is impossible to please God, for he who comes to God must believe that He is, and that He is a rewarder of those who diligently seek Him.
Romans 14:23 Whatsoever is not of faith is sin.
Ephesians 2:8 For by grace you have been saved through faith, and that not of yourselves; it is the gift of God.
Romans 3:26 To demonstrate at the present time His righteousness, that He might be just and the justifier of the one who has faith in Jesus.
Romans 5:1 Therefore being justified by faith, we have peace with God through our Lord Jesus Christ.
Romans 3:28 Therefore we conclude that a man is justified by faith without the deeds of the law.

Do You Believe in the Power of God to Do the Impossible?

Are You a Creationist or an Evolutionist?

Will God Create in You a New Heart?
Or Evolve Your Heart Over Time?

We read in Genesis that God said, "Let there be light," and there it was instantaneously at the power of His voice. That is creation.

Creation: belief that the power of God's voice creates something instantaneously from nothing
Evolution: belief that power in an object slowly over time improves itself
Theistic Evolution: belief that the power of God slowly over time creates/improves an object

2 Corinthians 5:17 Therefore, if anyone is in Christ, he is a new creation; old things have passed away; behold, all things have become new.

As we will see in this study, God is very clear that true conversion involves a total decided change from sin to righteousness. It is a new birth. We must have faith to believe God can create us anew instantaneously. Then we live out that faith – moment by moment surrendering and abiding in Christ. Thus, He creates us anew, writes His law upon our heart and mind, and gives us a desire to do His will.

RH March 10, 1904 He who has not sufficient faith in Christ to believe that He can keep him from sinning, has not the faith that will give him an entrance into the kingdom of God.

Impossible? No, but MIRACULOUS!!!!
That is the Power of Creation!

Growing in Christ and Sin Are Incompatible

As my husband and I were studying this subject together, we sat down one evening and begin to sketch - in an attempt to figure out the relationship between growing in Christ, and yet still sinning. The sketch and quotes brought clarity to our minds. At one point my husband said, "Growing in Christ and sin are incompatible!" This chart brought clarity to us, and our friends and family loved it too.

"The condition of eternal life is now just what it always has been, – just what it was in Paradise before the fall of our first parents, – perfect obedience to the law of God, perfect righteousness. If eternal life was granted on any condition short of this, then the happiness of the whole universe would be imperiled. The way would be open for sin, with all its train of woe & misery to be immortalized.

*It was possible for Adam, **before the fall, to form a righteous character by obedience to God's law.** But because he failed to do this, and because of his sin, our natures are fallen and we cannot make ourselves righteous. Since we are sinful, unholy, we cannot perfectly obey the holy law. We have no righteousness of our own with which to meet the claims of the law of God. But Christ made a way of escape for us. If you give yourself to Him, and accept Him as your Saviour, then sinful as your life **may have been,** for His sake you are accounted righteous.*

__More than this, Christ changes your heart. He abides in your heart by faith and the continual surrender of your will to Him; and so long as you do this, He will work in you to will and to do according to His good pleasure. Then with Christ working in you, you will manifest the same spirit and do the same good works – works of righteousness, obedience.__" Steps to Christ p.62-63

Growing in Christ & Sin Are Incompatible

There are different levels of sin I can sink into, but all sin is sin, binds me to Satan, and reproduces His character within me.

Like Satan ◄── **Sinning = Growing in Satan**

There are different depths of knowledge of Christ I can grow in, but when my heart is 100% submitted to Christ, I live His perfect obedience, am bound to Him, and He reproduces His character within me.

Faith (Submit + Obey) = Growing in Christ ──► **Like Christ**

5 Foolish Virgins lost because only partially filled with oil (Holy Spirit). Submitted to Holy Spirit sometimes, but not fully – all the time. ◄═ (See Page 155)

"Whoever commits sin also commits lawlessness, and sin is lawlessness. And you know that He was manifested to take away our sins, and in Him there is no sin. **Whoever sins has neither seen Him nor known Him.** *Little children, let no one deceive you. He who practices righteousness is righteous, just as He is righteous.* **He who sins is of the devil,** *for the devil has sinned from the beginning. For this purpose the Son of God was manifested, that He might destroy the works of the devil.* **Whoever has been born of God does not sin, for His seed remains in him; and he cannot sin, because he has been born of God."** *1 John 3:4-9*

9

I Believe:

1. Sin is of Satan – when we sin, we are allegiant to Satan and are growing in him.

2. Righteousness is of Christ – when we abide in Christ, we live His righteousness and grow in Him.

3. Christ offers us His gift of perfection – to live it out daily – by daily and moment by moment surrender of my will, asking to hear His voice guide me, and promising and following through to perfectly obey His voice.

4. Sanctification is both an act and an action. I am sanctified when I wholeheartedly surrender my entire life to Him. I then live out the process of sanctification by continuing to walk with Him in perfect obedience. I am continually growing in knowledge and an intimate relationship with Christ. Another way we grow is through living the sanctified life of obedience; our habits (neural pathways) change and the desire to sin diminishes and dies. We can also grow by getting rid of things in our lives that aren't immoral sins, but that take up time and money we could use in better ways for Christ.

5. Sanctification and sin are incompatible. I cannot be in the process of sanctification while committing a sin because if I sin, I have stepped out of the rulership of Christ and am living and promoting the character of Satan.

7. The requirement for heaven is perfect obedience which is only found in complete submission and obedience to God moment by moment. What ruined heaven the first time was Satan committed an unknown sin. This destroyed the perfect country of purity, love, and happiness. God will not allow sin back into heaven again – either known or unknown – because it would destroy heaven again. In and of our own knowledge and power, we can never be perfect. The only way to achieve the perfect obedience required for heaven is to be completely and perfectly submitted to Christ moment by moment. This is the only way the angels who live in heaven continue to live in perfection – by continually submitting the will, listening, and obeying.

The more I study, every Bible verse points to these simple and basic truths. Yet I have been blinded and deceived for years. We tend to read the word of God through the lens of human reasoning. But 99% God's truth + 1% human reasoning = 100% Satan's deceptive lie.

We have used our human reasoning to think as long as we are on the path toward Christ, and are progressively sinning less, we are saved. Yet this is still living in our own strength and not completely submitting to Christ. I am not safe walking toward Christ; (although that is a much better place to be than walking away from Him! - and hopefully that will finally lead to Him if I continue and there is enough time!) I am ONLY SAFE BY BEING IN CHRIST!!!! And I can be in Christ in one second. By simply surrendering my will. And I can do that now. And through His power I can continue to live in surrender.

As long as we preach progressively sinning less - we are not preaching Christ. Because I can progressively sin less in my own power - I've been doing a great job of it for 41 years. In that light – I have been perfect and successful. But when I realized that perfection was required – this caused me to see my need of Christ and surrender completely to Him. It caused me to realize I didn't need to just look to Christ, or be walking toward Christ, or need Christ's help: my only option was to completely die to self and completely fall into the arms of an all-loving and all-powerful God.

I thought I was converted years ago; I thought conversion was saying, "I love Jesus and want Him to live in my life." I thought it was slowly but surely experiencing victory over sin. But I have now finally been converted: I have surrendered my entire life to Jesus. I have died. He is alive. And it is the most glorious life I have ever experienced.

My Story of Learning to Abide in Christ

I was raised to love Jesus. From my youngest moments, Jesus was part of my life. I was taught to persevere and let nothing stop me. After great achievements, and still not finding happiness, I rebelled and went into the world. My life became full of addictions, and it is only by the mercy of God my life was spared.

When I became pregnant with my first child, I stopped drugs cold turkey. I loved my child growing inside of me so much, I was willing to do whatever was best for him. This took a lot of self-control, I struggled with the addiction and desire for drugs for years, but I just stubbornly stuck it out. Through the years, I used my stubbornness and self-control to slowly but surely resist and control my actions so I would do what was right. I found the temptations would diminish over time, but it took a lot of self-control and time to overcome. It seemed I was never free.

Several years ago, I was convicted I needed to be reading my Bible every day. As I did this, I began realizing I needed to be listening to the Holy Spirit and obeying His voice every day. I did my best for years – and this resulted in considerable changes in my life of putting away sin. But there was still something missing. My heart was still unreliable – so many times I would accidentally fail and sin again. It seemed in trials my emotions would just carry me away.

The Holy Spirit began to ask me some hard questions. "Lisa, how long are you going to sin? At what age will you finally overcome? How much time is enough to overcome? Would a loving God call you to a standard you cannot meet, and allow you to continue in sin and bondage, or deliver you completely?"

In 2017 I read an article by A.T. Jones that said Christ used the power of His Word to create instantaneously. God said, "Let there be light," and it immediately was. The

Bible says: "Create in me a new heart." Jones challenged: are we a creationist or an evolutionist? Do I believe God has the power, through His Word, to create in me a clean heart immediately – or do I believe God is an evolutionist and will slowly change me from sinner to child of God. I knew I was a creationist and believed God's power, but I didn't know how to live out my belief. But the seed was planted.

In January of 2021 my mom gave me a book: *The Guide to Christian Perfection* by Fitch. For the first time, I saw Bible verses that proved it possible to live a perfect life in Christ. I couldn't deny the Biblical evidence; now I believed. But I didn't know how to make it a reality in my life.

In April of 2021, our family went through a series of challenging crises, that showed me "a little tiny normal sin that we all do" results in terrible sin if not completely eradicated from the life. As a family we determined to have a revival and reformation and completely submit to Christ and cleanse our lives of sin. Grand improvement was made, but sometimes we would find ourselves back in sin. We each seemed stuck in a cycle: repent – obey for awhile – sin….

In September 2021, I was gifted *The Life of Victory* by Macguire and read another book teaching victory. A week later, I was gifted the book *Christ Our Righteousness* by Bill Lehman. I read the entire book that week. I read that in my own strength I will always be a sinner, but I only need invite Christ to come live inside of me and live His life within me, and I would thus be converted and live the sanctified life. It seemed too good to be true. I checked it with scripture and found it to be true. My family in Christ found it to be Biblically true also.

After a Bible study in January 2022, I realized I needed to study the Bible alone on this subject more deeply. I read, "He who abides in Christ does not sin." (1 John 3:6) In that sentence I realized I was not fine. My big sins were gone. My outward sin was gone most of the time. But my mind still raged with negative thoughts. Eventually my thoughts would take over, leading me to sin through impatience, frustration, worry, etc. I thought I was abiding, and so this verse didn't make any sense to me – but I realized I had a problem – and there must be a solution in the Word of God.

In an effort to better understand abiding in Christ, I began to categorize verses by different aspects. I did this all day for several days and came to a stunning reality: when I abide in Christ, daily and moment by moment listening to the Holy Spirit and surrendering my will, I cannot sin. I grow in Christ by obeying. Every time I sin, I become more like Satan. The two are direct opposites. Growing in Christ and sin are incompatible. I found there was a common theme of complete surrender to God that resulted in complete and immediate transformation such as the new birth of John 3, Acts 2:37-43 when 3,000 were converted, the life of Saul turned to Paul, and the disciples after Christ was crucified and resurrected. I found a principle of dying to self and receiving everything through Christ as in the vine in John 15. Could it be this simple? Could it be I had been using my own power all these years to slowly change and obey the law, and yet Christ could truly instantaneously change me and give me complete and full victory?

And so, I stepped out in faith, believing it was true. I committed to surrender my entire life to Christ – every action and every thought. I began to do this daily before I got out of bed each morning saying something like: "In and of myself there is nothing good, and today I choose to die to self and ask You to live inside of me. Fill me with Your Spirit, love for You, and Your love for others. Speak to me and guide me all day long and I promise to listen to that voice and immediately obey." I then spent an hour reading God's word and praying. My life was truly instantly transformed from the inside. The addictions that previously plagued me, lost their power. My thoughts were on Christ. I felt a peace, joy, and freedom I had never experienced before.

I still had temptation. I would be tempted to eat something I shouldn't, or a negative thought would pop into my mind. But now that I knew how to resist the devil, I would simply stop, and say, "Father, I submit this desire to you. Please take it away. I desire to be healthy and to live for your honor and glory." I would then walk away and go do something else and the desire would leave. When a negative thought popped into my head I would stop and pray, "Father, I submit my will to you. I do not want to think this negative thought, please take it from me and please fill my mind with Your thoughts of thankfulness. Please fill me with Your comfort." By faith I would then begin to praise God and the negativity would immediately leave and I would feel God's comfort and power.

I think many of us seeking Christ have focused on perfection. But in ourselves we can never be perfect. We are not called to perfection, but rather we are called to perfect obedience. There is a distinct difference. Perfection is from our knowledge and self-control. Perfect Obedience is from the knowledge of God, a heart of faith and trust, and surrender of will to the voice of the Holy Spirit who is always guiding us. That is obtainable right now, moment by moment, and for eternity.

My prayers have radically changed. Instead of "Please help me," I now pray "Fill me with Your love, Your truth, live out Your life within me, Fill me with Your words," etc. Instead of viewing myself as the leader and God as the counselor to help me, I view Him living inside of me – Him as the leader – and my mind and body simply living out His life. Our part in the new birth is simple: a continual complete surrender of will and desire for God's will. A new instantaneous birth is real. God is alive and willing to live within. He will fill every hole in our heart and mind and we will be satisfied and overflowing.

"O taste and see that the Lord is good."
Psalms 34:8

God: The Perfect Father

I didn't have a perfect father. I haven't been a perfect mother. And so I grew up, and we all grow up, with a skewed vision of God as Father, and presenting a skewed vision of God.

I remember one day specifically praying to God, "I know in my brain you are my perfect Father, but I don't feel You! How do you say You are my Father when you don't do what a Father does!" Looking back on that experience, I think He was saying, "I am your Father – I'm right here – waiting for you to come to Me and abide in Me. I'm waiting for you to take your eyes of self and put them on Me. I'm waiting for you to stop living your life your way and trust Me." This was all happening simultaneously to my studying how to abide in Christ.

As the Holy Spirit worked on my heart, and guided me into more and more truth, my life began to change. The more I listened to His voice, the more my life changed, and the greater peace and joy I experienced. It didn't take the trials away, but rather I began to view the trials as a blessing – a way to experience God to a deeper level.

I remember after one particularly challenging but victorious day, I laid down to sleep. God said, "Lisa – I am your perfect Father. Do you feel Me now?" And I had to break down in tears of joy. Yes, I had now found my heavenly Father. I had found a Father who always guided me in all ways throughout the day, who warned me of dangers, who protected me from dangers too complex for me to understand, who chastened me in love when I stepped out of line, and who comforted and soothed my emotions. I had found a Father who I could feel His presence, hear His voice, and who listened to me. Wow, what a day that was!

When I view my heavenly Father, I experience a Father who loves me – the true definition of love – not my previously screwed up definition of worldly love. He loves me so much that He protects me from dangers I am not aware of. For example, when my boys were very little, I kept them back from the hot wood stove, because they didn't understand the danger, no matter how many words I used. I believe God protects me even from the sin I don't know about! Because a truly loving Father protects His children from all harm if we will listen to Him and obey. I experience a Father who is always watching out for me. I tried to do that for my little boys – but sometimes I couldn't see danger coming! I experience a Father who judges justly. If I am in sin, He deals me fair consequences so I will learn to see the awfulness of sin and see my need for Him to rescue me. He also comforts me when being mistreated and tells me to pick my head up and remember I am a child of the King of the Universe. But what I love about my Heavenly Father the most: He's always there. I don't have to call Him or drive to visit Him – He is always present to give me His guidance and love. I never thought it possible – but I truly have found an intimate relationship with my heavenly Father. I feel His presence. My Father God is real – and I am willing to lose everything – as long as I still have Him.

Salvation:
God Initiates – We Respond

God's Part	Our Part
He will draw us	Do not resist His drawing
He will convict us of sin, righteousness, and judgement	Acknowledge our guilt and need of His righteousness
He will give us repentance	Confess and forsake our sins and give Him our heart
He will forgive, cleanse, regenerate, and free us to live the sanctified life	Believe and accept
He will live in us and empower us	Live by faith and bear much fruit
He will make a way of escape when we are tempted	Take God's way of escape and submit to Him
He will be our advocate if we fall	Repent and turn back to Him

*** Taken from *What Shall I Do To Inherit Eternal Life?*
By Margaret Davis***

How to Abide in Christ
These Steps are to be done DAILY
as well as when we sin

"If anyone desires to come after Me, let him deny himself, and take up his cross **daily**, and follow Me." Luke 9:23

"I affirm, by the boasting in you which I have in Christ Jesus our Lord, I die **daily**." 1 Corinthians 15:31

"If we have walked with God in fellowship of the Spirit, it is because we have sought Him **daily** by faith." RH March 2, 1897

1. Realize My Need
Romans 7:24 "O wretched man that I am!"
SC 28 "The same divine mind that is working upon the things of nature is speaking to the hearts of men and creating an inexpressible craving for something they have not....The Spirit of God is pleading with them to seek for those things that alone can give peace and rest – the grace of Christ, the joy of holiness."

2. Acknowledge God as my Loving Ruler
Psalms 78:35 "Then they remembered that God was their rock, and the Most High God their Redeemer."
SC27 "Christ manifested a love that is incomprehensible; and as the sinner beholds this love, it softens the heart, impresses the mind, and inspires contrition in the soul."

3. Come to Christ as I Am in Prayer
Matthew 9:13 "I did not come to call the righteous, but sinners, to repentance."
SC 31 "If you see your sinfulness, do not wait to make yourself better.... We must come to Christ just as we are."

4. Repent and Turn From Evil

1 John 1:9 "If we confess our sins, He is faithful and just to forgive us our sins, and to cleanse us from all unrighteousness."

SC 23 "Repentance includes sorrow for sin and a turning away from it. We shall not renounce sin unless we see its sinfulness; until we turn away from it in heart, there will be no real change in the life."

5. Submit my Will and Choose God's Will

James 7:17 "If anyone wills to do His will, he shall know."

SC 48 "By yielding up your will to Christ, you ally yourself with the power that is above all principalities and powers."

6. Tune Into Holy Spirit's Impressions and God's Word

Jude 1:24 "Now unto Him who is able to keep you from falling, and to present you faultless before the presence of His glory with exceeding joy."

SC 47-48 "Desire for goodness and holiness are right as far as they go; but if you stop here, they will avail nothing. Many will be lost while hoping and desiring to be Christians. They do not come to the point of yielding the will to God. They do not now choose to be Christians. Through the right exercise of the will, an entire change may be made in your life. By yielding up your will to Christ, you ally yourself with the power that is above all principalities and powers. You will have strength from above to hold you steadfast, and thus through your constant surrender to God you will be enabled to live the new life, even the life of faith."

7. If We Fail and Sin – Come to Jesus Again

1 John 2:1 "My little children, these things I write to you, that you may not sin. And if anyone sins, we have an Advocate with the Father, Jesus Christ the righteous."

Proverbs 24:16 "For a righteous man may fall seven times and rise again, but the wicked shall fall by calamity."

How to Abide in Christ When Tempted

"Therefore submit to God. Resist the devil and he will flee from you. Draw near to God and He will draw near to you. Cleanse your hands, you sinners, and purify your hearts, you double-minded."
James 4:7-8

"I saw how grace could be obtained. Go to your closet, and there alone plead with God: "Create in me a clean heart, O God; and renew a right spirit within me." Be in earnest, be sincere. Fervent prayer availeth much. Jacoblike, wrestle in prayer. Agonize. Jesus, in the garden, sweat great drops of blood; you must make an effort. Do not leave your closet until you feel strong in God; then watch, and just as long as you watch and pray you can keep these evil besetments under, and the grace of God can appear and will appear in you." – 1T 158

1. "Therefore submit to God."
Say, "God, I want and choose to love you, trust you, and cheerfully obey your voice through your power."

2. "Resist the devil and he will flee from you."
Say, "Get Behind Me Satan!"

3. "Draw near to God and He will draw near to you."
Sing a hymn, read His word, praise Him, thank Him for His victory.

4. "Cleanse your hands."
Get rid of everything associated with the sinful habit. Cleanse your home and everything you own.

5. "Purify your hearts, you double-minded"

Do not be double-minded by thinking about sin and God. We act out what we think. Choose to reject all thoughts of sin at first thought, and "bringing every thought into captivity to the obedience of Christ," (2 Corinthians 10:5) think only God's truth and God's love.

"When Jesus came into the world, Satan's power was turned against Him. From the time when He appeared as a babe in Bethlehem, the usurper worked to bring about His destruction. In every possible way he sought to prevent Jesus from developing a perfect childhood, a faultless manhood, a holy ministry, and an unblemished sacrifice. But he was defeated. He could not lead Jesus into sin. He could not discourage Him, or drive Him from a work He had come on earth to do. From the desert to Calvary, the storm of Satan's wrath beat upon Him, but the more mercilessly it fell, the more firmly did the Son of God cling to the hand of His Father, and press on in the bloodstained path. All the efforts of Satan to oppress and overcome Him only brought out in a purer light His spotless character."
DA 759

Chapter 1
Christ Came to Take Away Sin

Daniel 9:24 70 weeks are determined for your people and for your holy city, to finish the transgression, to make an end of sins, to make reconciliation for iniquity, to bring in everlasting righteousness.

Matthew 1:21 And you shall call His name Jesus, for He will save His people from their sins.

Luke 4:18-19 The Spirit of the Lord is upon Me, because He has appointed Me to preach the gospel to the poor; He has sent Me to heal the brokenhearted, to proclaim liberty to the captives and recovery of sight to the blind, to set at liberty those who are oppressed.

Luke 5:32 I have not come to call the righteous, but sinners to repentance.

John 1:29 Behold! The Lamb of God who takes away the sin of the world!

John 16:8 And when He has come, He will convict the world of sin, and of righteousness, and of judgment.

1 Timothy 1:15 Christ Jesus came into the world to save sinners; of whom I am chief.

1 John 3:8-9 He who sins is of the devil, for the devil has sinned from the beginning. For this purpose the Son of God was manifested, that He might destroy the works of the devil. Whoever has been born of God does not sin, for His seed remains in him; and he cannot sin, because he has been born of God.

RH April 24, 1900 We must learn of Christ. We must know what He is to those He has ransomed. We must realize that through belief in Him it is our privilege to be partakers of the divine nature, and so escape the corruption that is in the world through lust. Then we are cleansed from all sin, all defects of character. We need not retain one sinful propensity. Christ is the sinbearer; John pointed the people to Him, saying, "Behold the Lamb of God, which taketh away the sin of the world."

1SM 396   He presents me to God in the spotless garment of which no thread was woven by any human agent. All is of Christ, and all the glory, honor, and majesty are to be given to the Lamb of God, which taketh away the sins of the world.

DA 38   None but Christ can fashion anew the character that has been ruined by sin. He came to expel the demons that had controlled the will.

DA 466   Christ came to break the shackles of sin-slavery from the soul. "If the Son therefore shall make you free, ye shall be free indeed."

COL 419, 420   The religion of Christ means more than forgiveness of sin; it means taking away our sins, and filling the vacuum with the graces of the Holy Spirit.

EW 209   When the soldier pierced the side of Jesus as He hung upon the cross, there came out two distinct streams, one of blood, the other of water. The blood was to wash away the sins of those who should believe in His name, and the water was to represent that living water which is obtained from Jesus to give life to the believer.

4T 251   Jesus died, not to save man *in* his sins, but *from* his sins. Man is to leave the error of his ways, to follow the example of Christ, to take up his cross and follow Him, denying self, and obeying God at any cost.

Chapter 2
Christ Submitted and
Formed Righteous Character

John 6:38   For I have come down from heaven, not to do My own will, but the will of Him who sent Me.

John 17:19   And for their sakes I sanctify Myself, that they also may be sanctified by the truth.

Hebrews 2:10   For it was fitting for Christ, for whom are all things and by whom are all things, in bringing many sons to glory, to make the author of their salvation perfect through sufferings. [Christ never sinned, yet was still made perfect]

Hebrews 2:18   For in that He Himself has suffered, being tempted, He is able to aid those who are tempted.

Hebrews 5:7-9   Who, in the days of His flesh, when He had offered up prayers and supplications, with vehement cries and tears to Him who was able to save Him from death, and was heard because of His godly fear, though He was a Son, yet he learned obedience by the things which He suffered. And having been perfected, He became the author of eternal salvation to all who obey Him.

Luke 22:42   Saying, "Father, if it is Your will, remove this cup away from Me; nevertheless not My will, but Yours, be done."

Philippians 2:5-8   Let this mind be in you which was also in Christ Jesus, who, being in the form of God, did not consider it robbery to be equal with God, but made Himself of no reputation, taking the form of a bondservant, and coming in the likeness of men. And being found in appearance as a man, He humbled Himself and became obedient to the point of death, even the death of the cross.

1 Peter 2:21-23   Because Christ also suffered for us, leaving us an example, that you should follow His steps: "Who committed no sin, nor was deceit found in His mouth," who, when He was reviled, did not revile in return; when He suffered, He did not threaten, but committed Himself to Him who judges righteously.

Revelation 3:21 To him who overcomes I will grant to sit with Me on My throne, as I also overcame and sat down with My Father on His throne.

DA 130 Jesus gained the victory through submission and faith in God.

DA 389 As the Son of God lived by faith in the Father, so are we to live by faith in Christ. So fully was Jesus surrendered to the will of God that the Father alone appeared in His life. Although tempted in all points like as we are, He stood before the world untainted by the evil that surrounded Him. Thus we also are to overcome as Christ overcame.

TMK 34 We must look to Christ; we must resist as He resisted; we must pray as He prayed; we must agonize as He agonized, if we would conquer as He conquered.

MH 479 Christ in His life on earth made no plans for Himself. He accepted God's plans for Him, and day by day the Father unfolded His plans. So should we depend upon God, that our lives may be the simple outworking of His will. As we commit our ways to Him, He will direct our steps.

MB 21 To Jesus, who emptied Himself for the salvation of lost humanity, the Holy Spirit was given without measure. So it will be given to every follower of Christ when the whole heart is surrendered for His indwelling. Out Lord Himself has given the command, "Be filled with the Spirit." Eph 5:18

ST October 29, 1894 Jesus Christ is our example in all things. He began life, passed through its experience, and ended its record, with a sanctified human will. He was tempted in all points like as we are, and yet because He kept His will surrendered and sanctified, He never bent in the slightest degree toward the doing of evil, or toward manifesting rebellion against God.

ST May 10, 1899 Amid impurity, Christ maintained His purity. Satan could not stain or corrupt it. His character revealed a perfect hatred for sin. It was His holiness that stirred against Him all the passion of a profligate world; for by His perfect life He threw upon the world a perpetual reproach, and made manifest the contrast between transgression and the pure, spotless righteousness of One that knew no sin.

1T 339-340 Jesus, considered as a man, was perfect, yet He grew in grace. "And Jesus increased in wisdom and stature, and in favor with God and man." Even the most perfect Christian may increase continually in the knowledge and love of God.

Chapter 3
We Are Born Sinners

Job 14:4 Who can bring a clean thing out of an unclean? No one!

Isaiah 64:6 But we are all like an unclean thing, and all our righteousnesses are like filthy rags; we all fade as a leaf, and our iniquities, like the wind, have taken us away.

Jeremiah 13:23 Can the Ethiopian change his skin, or the leopard his spots? Then may you also do good, who are accustomed to do evil.

John 15:5 Without me ye can do nothing.

Romans 3:10-12 There is none righteous, no, not one; there is none who understands; there is none who seeks after God, they have all turned aside; they have together become unprofitable; there is none who does good, no, not one.

Romans 7:24 O wretched man that I am! Who shall deliver me from this body of death?

Romans 8:7 Because the carnal mind is enmity against God; for it is not subject to the law of God, nor indeed can be.

Romans 10:3-4 For they being ignorant of God's righteousness, and seeking to establish their own righteousness, have not submitted to the righteousness of God. For Christ is the end of the law for righteousness to everyone who believes.

1 Corinthians 2:14 The natural man does not receive the things of the Spirit of God, for they are foolishness to him: nor can he know them, because they are spiritually discerned.

SC 18 It is impossible for us, of ourselves, to escape from the pit of sin in which we are sunken. Our hearts are evil and we cannot change them.

SC 18 Education, culture, the exercise of the will, human effort, all have their proper sphere, but here they are powerless. They may produce an outward correctness of behavior, but they cannot change the heart, they cannot purify the springs of life.

SC 21   In vain are men's dreams of progress, in vain all efforts for the uplifting of humanity, if they neglect the One Source of hope and help for the fallen race.

SC 28-29   When the light from Christ shines into our souls, we shall see how impure we are; we shall discern selfishness of motive, the enmity against God, that has defiled every act of life. Then we shall know that our own righteousness is indeed as filthy rags, and that the blood of Christ alone can cleanse us from the defilement of sin, and renew our hearts in His own likeness.

SC 69   Many have an idea that they must do some part of the work alone.   They have trusted in Christ for the forgiveness of sin, but now they seek by their own efforts to live aright.   But every such effort must fail. Jesus said, "Without Me ye can do nothing."

1SM 353-354   Some who come to God by repentance and confession, and even believe that their sins are forgiven, still fail of claiming, as they should, the promises of God. They do not see that Jesus is an ever-present Saviour; and they are not ready to commit the keeping of their souls to Him, relying upon Him to perfect the work of grace begun in their hearts. While they are committing themselves to God, there is a great deal of self-dependence.   There are conscientious souls that trust partly to God, and partly to themselves. They do not look to God, to be kept by His power, but depend upon watchfulness against temptation, and the performance of certain duties for acceptance with Him.   There are no victories in this kind of faith.   Such persons toil to no purpose; their souls are in continual bondage, and they find no rest until their burdens are laid at the feet of Jesus. There is need of constant watchfulness, and of earnest loving devotion; but these will come naturally when the soul is kept by the power of God through faith.   We can do nothing, absolutely nothing, to commend ourselves to divine favor. We must not trust at all to ourselves nor to our good works; but when as erring, sinful beings we come to Christ, we may find rest in His love.

1SM 364   He who is trying to reach heaven by his own works in keeping the law, is attempting an impossibility. Man cannot be saved without obedience, but his works should not be of himself; Christ should work in him to will and to do of His good pleasure. If a man could save himself by his own works, he might have something in himself in which to rejoice.

DA 38   None but Christ can fashion anew the character that has been ruined by sin.

TM 456   None but God can subdue the pride of man's heart. We cannot save ourselves. We cannot regenerate ourselves…. What is justification by faith? It is the work of God in laying the glory of man in the dust, and doing for man that which is it not in his power to do for himself.

Chapter 4
Don't Despair in Sin – Come to Jesus

2 Chronicles 30:9 For the LORD your God is gracious and merciful, and will not turn His face from you if you return to Him.

Ezekiel 18:30-32 "Therefore I will judge you, O house of Israel, every one according to his ways," says the Lord God. "Repent, and turn from all your transgressions, so that iniquity will not be your ruin. Cast away from you all the transgressions which you have committed, and get yourselves a new heart and a new spirit. For why should you die, O house of Israel? For I have no pleasure in the death of one who dies," says the Lord GOD. "Therefore turn and live!"

Matthew 11:28-30 Come to Me, all you who labor and are heavy laden, and I will give you rest. Take My yoke upon you and learn from Me, for I am gentle and lowly in heart, and you will find rest for your souls. For My yoke is easy and My burden is light.

Mark 10:26-27 And they were greatly astonished beyond measure, saying among themselves, "Who then can be saved?" But looking at them Jesus said, "With men it is impossible, but not with God; for with God all things are possible."

Acts 3:19 Repent therefore and be converted, that your sins may be blotted out, so that times of refreshing may come from the presence of the Lord.

Hebrews 12:1-3 Therefore we also, since we are surrounded by so great a cloud of witnesses, let us lay aside every weight, and the sin which so easily ensnares us, and let us run with endurance the race that is set before us, looking unto Jesus, the author and finisher of our faith, who for the joy that was set before Him endured the cross, despising the shame, and has sat down at the right hand of the throne of God. For consider Him who endured such hostility from sinners against Himself, lest you become weary and discouraged in your souls.

2 Peter 3:9 The Lord... is longsuffering toward us, not willing that any should perish but that all should come to repentance.

1 John 2:1 These things I write to you, that you may not sin. And if anyone sins, we have an Advocate with the Father, Jesus Christ the righteous.

GW 160 The way that God has provided is so complete, so perfect, that man cannot, by any works that he can do, add to its perfection. It is broad enough to receive the most hardened sinner, if he truly repents, and yet so narrow that in it sin can find no place. This is the path cast up for the ransomed of the Lord to walk in.

SC 35 As you see the enormity of sin, as you see yourself as you really are, do not give up to despair. It was sinners that Christ came to save.

SC 36 Acknowledge your sin, but tell the enemy that "Christ Jesus came into the world to save sinners" and that you may be saved by His matchless love.

MH 85 The sense of sin has poisoned the springs of life. But Christ says, "I will take your sins; I will give you peace. I have bought you with My blood. You are Mine. My grace shall strengthen your weakened will; your remorse for sin I will remove." When temptations assail you, when care and perplexity surround you, when, depressed and discouraged, you are ready to yield to despair, look to Jesus, and the darkness that encompasses you will be dispelled by the bright shining of His presence. When sin struggles for the mastery in your soul, and burdens the conscience, look to the Saviour. His grace is sufficient to subdue sin. Let your grateful heart, trembling with uncertainty, turn to Him. Lay hold on the hope set before you. Christ waits to adopt you into His family. His strength will help your weakness; He will lead you step by step. Place your hand in His, and let Him guide you.

SC 52-53 We may come with all our weakness, our folly, our sinfulness, and fall at His feet in penitence. It is His glory to encircle us in the arms of His love and to bind up our wounds, to cleanse us from all impurity…. None are so sinful that they cannot find strength, purity, and righteousness in Jesus, who died for them. He is waiting to strip them of their garments stained and polluted with sin, and to put upon them the white robes of righteousness; He bids them live and not die.

SC 64 There are those who have known the pardoning love of Christ and who really desire to be children of God, yet they realize that their character is imperfect, their life faulty, and they are ready to doubt whether their hearts have been renewed by the Holy Spirit. To such I would say, Do not draw back in despair. We shall often have to bow down and weep at the feet of Jesus because of our shortcomings and mistakes, but we are not to be discouraged. Even if we are overcome by the enemy, we are not cast off, not forsaken and rejected of God. No; Christ is at the right hand of God, who also maketh intercession for us. Said the beloved John, "These things write I unto you, that ye sin not. And if any man sin, we have an advocate with the Father, Jesus Christ the righteous." 1 John 2:1…. He desires to restore you to Himself, to see His own purity and holiness reflected in you. And if you will but yield yourself to Him, He that hath begun a good work in you will carry it forward to the day of Jesus Christ. Pray more fervently; believe more fully. As we come to distrust our own power, let us trust the power of our Redeemer, and we shall praise Him who is the health of our countenance.

SC 64-65 The closer you come to Jesus, the more faulty you will appear in your own eyes; for your vision will be clearer, and your imperfections will be seen in broad and distinct contrast to His perfect nature. This is evidence that Satan's delusions have lost their power; that the vivifying influence of the Spirit of God is arousing you. No deep-seated love for Jesus can dwell in the heart that does not realize its own sinfulness. The soul that is transformed by the grace of Christ will admire His divine character; but if we do not see our own moral deformity, it is unmistakable evidence that we have not had a view of the beauty and excellence of Christ.... A view of our sinfulness drives us to Him who can pardon; and when the soul, realizing its helplessness, reaches out after Christ, He will reveal Himself in power. The more our sense of need drives us to Him and to the word of God, the more exalted views we shall have of His character, and the more fully we shall reflect His image.

1SM 325 How willing is Christ to take possession of the soul temple if we will let Him! He is represented as waiting and knocking at the door of the heart. Then why does He not enter? It is because the love of sin has closed the door to the heart. As soon as we consent to give sin up, to acknowledge our guilt, the barrier is removed between the soul and the Savior.

1SM 350-351 God does not give us up because of our sins. We may make mistakes, and grieve His Spirit; but when we repent, and come to Him with contrite hearts, He will not turn us away. There are hindrances to be removed. Wrong feelings have been cherished, and there have been pride, self-sufficiency, impatience, and murmurings. All these separate us from God. Sins must be confessed; there must be a deeper work of grace in the heart.... We have long desired and tried to obtain these blessings, but have not received them because we have cherished the idea that we could do something to make ourselves worthy of them. We have not looked away from ourselves, believing that Jesus is a living Saviour.

1SM 352 Although millions who need to be healed will reject His offered mercy, not one who trusts in His merits will be left to perish. While we realize our helpless condition without Christ, we must not be discouraged; we must rely upon a crucified and risen Saviour. Poor, sin-sick, discouraged soul, look and live. Jesus has pledged His word; He will save all who come unto Him. Come to Jesus, and receive rest and peace. You may have the blessing even now. Satan suggests that you are helpless and cannot bless yourself. It is true; you are helpless. But lift up Jesus before him.

1SM 353 Some seem to feel that they must be on probation and must prove to the Lord that they are reformed, before they can claim the blessing. But these dear souls may claim the blessing even now. They must have His grace, the Spirit of Christ, to help their infirmities, or they cannot form a Christian character. Jesus loves to have us come to Him, just as we are – sinful, helpless, dependent.

COL 156 It is Satan's special device to lead man into sin, and then leave him, helpless and trembling, fearing to seek for pardon.

PK 276 God allows men a period of probation; but there is a point beyond which divine patience is exhausted, and the judgments of God are sure to follow. The Lord bears long with men, and with cities, mercifully giving warnings to save them from divine wrath; but a time will come when pleadings for mercy will no longer be heard, and the rebellious element that continues to reject the light of truth will be blotted out, in mercy to themselves and to those who would otherwise be influenced by their example.

Chapter 5
<u>Surrender of Will Required</u>

Proverbs 23:26   My son, give me your heart, and let your eyes observe my ways.

Matthew 16:24-26   Then Jesus said to His disciples, "If anyone desires to come after Me, let him deny himself, and take up his cross, and follow Me. For whoever desires to save his life will lose it, but whoever loses his life for My sake will find it. For what is a man profited if he gains the whole world, and loses his own soul? Or what will a man give in exchange for his soul?"

Mark 14:36   And He said, "Abba, Father, all things are possible for You. Take this cup away from Me; nevertheless, not what I will, but what You will."

Luke 14:33   Whoever of you does not forsake all that he has cannot be My disciple.

John 7:17   If any man wants to do His will, he shall know concerning the doctrine.

Romans 12:1   I beseech you therefore, brethren, by the mercies of God, that you present your bodies a living sacrifice, holy, acceptable to God, which is your reasonable service.

1 Corinthians 6:19-20   Or do you not know that your body is the temple of the Holy Spirit who is in you, whom you have from God, and you are not your own? For you were bought at a price; therefore glorify God in your body and in your spirit, which are God's.

2 Corinthians 5:15   He died for all, that those who live should live no longer for themselves, but for Him who died for them and rose again.

James 4:7   Therefore submit to God. Resist the devil and he will flee from you.

SC 43 God desires to heal us, to set us free. But since this requires an entire transformation, a renewing of our whole

37

nature, we must yield ourselves wholly to Him. The warfare against self is the greatest battle that was ever fought. The yielding of self, surrendering all to the will of God, requires a struggle; but the soul must submit to God before it can be renewed in holiness.

SC 46 But what do we give up, when we give all? A sin-polluted heart, for Jesus to purify, to cleanse by His own blood, and to save by His matchless love. And yet men think it hard to give up all! I am ashamed to hear it spoken of.

SC 47 Many are inquiring, "How am I to make the surrender of myself to God?" You desire to give yourself to Him, but you are weak in moral power, in slavery to doubt, and controlled by the habits of your life in sin. Your promises and resolutions are like ropes of sand. You cannot control your thoughts, your impulses, your affections. The knowledge of your broken promises and forfeited pledges weakens your confidence in your own sincerity, and causes you to feel that God cannot accept you; but you need not despair. What you need to understand is the true force of the will. This is the governing power in the nature of man, the power of decision, or of choice. Everything depends on the right action of the will. The power of choice God has given to men; it is theirs to exercise. You cannot change your heart, you cannot of yourself give to God its affections; but you can choose to serve Him. You can give Him your will; He will then work in you to will and to do according to His good pleasure. Thus your whole nature will be brought under control of the Spirit of Christ; your affections will be centered upon Him, your thoughts will be in harmony with Him.

SC 48 By yielding up your will to Christ, you ally yourself with the power that is above all principalities and powers. You will have strength from above to hold you steadfast, and thus through your constant surrender to God you will be enabled to live the new life, even the life of faith.

1SM 397   As God works in the heart, and man surrenders his will to God, and cooperates with God, he works out in the life what God works in by the Holy Spirit, and there is harmony between the purpose of the heart and the practice of the life. Every sin must be renounced as the hateful thing that crucified the Lord of life and glory, and the believer must have a progressive experience by continually doing the works of Christ. It is by continual surrender of the will, by continual obedience, that the blessing of justification is retained.

1SM 399-400   There are some who are seeking, always seeking, for the goodly pearl. But they do not make an entire surrender of their wrong habits. They do not die to self that Christ may live in them…. They never know what it is to have peace and harmony in the soul; for without entire surrender there is no rest, no joy. Almost Christians, yet not fully Christians, they seem near the kingdom of heaven, but they do not enter therein. Almost but not wholly saved means to be not almost but wholly lost.

AA 51   Holiness is not rapture: it is an entire surrender of the will to God; it is living by every word that proceeds from the mouth of God; it is doing the will of our heavenly Father; it is trusting God in trial, in darkness as well as in light; it is walking by faith and not by sight; it is relying on God with unquestioning confidence, and resting in His love.

DA 466   In the work of redemption there is no compulsion. No external force is employed. Under the influence of the Spirit of God, man is left free to choose whom he will serve. In the change that takes place when the soul surrenders to Christ, there is the highest sense of freedom. The expulsion of sin is the act of the soul itself True, we have no power to free ourselves from Satan's control; but when we desire to be set free from sin, and in our great need cry out for a power out of and above ourselves, the powers of the soul are imbued with the divine energy of the Holy Spirit, and they obey the dictates of the will in fulfilling the will of God.

DA 664   Jesus revealed no qualities, and exercised no powers, that men may not have through faith in Him. His perfect humanity is that which all His followers may possess, if they will be in subjection to God as He was.

DA 672   We cannot use the Holy Spirit. The Spirit is to use us. Through the Spirit God works in His people "to will and to do of his good pleasure." Phil 2:13. But many will not submit to this. They want to manage themselves. This is why they do not receive the heavenly gift.

MYP 30   To have the religion of Christ means that you have absolutely surrendered your all to God, and consented to the guidance of the Holy Spirit. Through the gift of the Holy Spirit moral power will be given you…. The surrender of all our powers to God greatly simplifies the problem of life. It weakens and cuts short a thousand struggles with the passions of the natural heart.

MYP 151   Pure religion has to do with the will. The will is the governing power in the nature of man, bringing all the other faculties under its sway. The will is not the taste or the inclination, but it is the deciding power, which works in the children of men unto obedience to God or unto disobedience.

MB 16   It is the love of self that destroys our peace. While self is all alive, we stand ready continually to guard it from mortification and insult; but when we are dead, and our life is hid with Christ in God, we shall not take neglects or slights to heart. We shall be deaf to reproach and blind to scorn and insult.

MB 143   We cannot retain self and yet enter the kingdom of God. If we ever attain unto holiness, it will be through the renunciation of self and the reception of the mind of Christ.

AA 565   The reason many in this age of the world make no greater advancement in the divine life is because they interpret the will of God to be just what they will to do. While following their own desires, they flatter themselves that they are conforming to God's will. These have no conflicts with self. There are others who for a time are successful in the struggle against their selfish desire for pleasure and ease. They are sincere and earnest, but grow weary of protracted effort, of daily death, of ceaseless turmoil. Indolence seems inviting, death to self repulsive; and they close their drowsy eyes, and fall under the power of temptation instead of resisting it.

COL 96 In all who will submit themselves to the Holy Spirit a new principle of life is to be implanted; the lost image of God is to be restored in humanity.

COL 188 Every one that will submit to be ransomed, Christ will rescue from the pit of corruption and from the briers of sin.

COL 411 The class represented by the foolish virgins are not hypocrites. They have a regard for the truth, they have advocated the truth, they are attracted to those who believe the truth; but they have not yielded themselves to the Holy Spirit's working. They have not fallen upon the Rock, Christ Jesus, and permitted their old nature to be broken up.... The Spirit works upon man's heart, according to his desire and consent implanting in him a new nature; but the class represented by the foolish virgins have been content with a superficial work. They do not know God.

1SM 110 When you give up your own will, your own wisdom, and learn of Christ, you will find admittance in the kingdom of God.

CD 35 The plan of beginning outside and trying to work inward has always failed and always will fail. God's plan with you is to begin at the seat of all difficulties, the heart, and then from out of the heart will issue the principles of righteousness; the reformation will be outward as well as inward.

DA 324 When the soul surrenders itself to Christ, a new power takes possession of the new heart. A change is wrought which man can never accomplish for himself. It is a supernatural work, bringing a supernatural element into human nature. The soul that is yielded to Christ becomes His own fortress, which He holds in a revolted world, and He intends that no authority shall be known in it but His own. A soul thus kept in possession by the heavenly agencies is impregnable to the assaults of Satan... The only defense against evil is the indwelling of Christ in the heart through faith in righteousness. Unless we become vitally connected with God, we can never resist the unhallowed effects of self-love, self-indulgence, and temptation to sin. We may leave off many bad habits, for the time we may part company with Satan; but without a vital connection with God, through the surrender of ourselves to Him moment by moment, we shall be overcome.

1T 158   If the heart is right, your words, your dress, your acts, will all be right.

2T 263   You cannot serve God and mammon. You are either wholly on the Lord's side or on on the side of the enemy.... Some persons make their religious life a failure because they are always wavering and do not have a determination. They are frequently convicted and come almost up to the point of surrendering all for God; but, failing to meet the point, they fall back again.

2T 425   Those who are dead to self will not feel so readily and will not be prepared to resist everything which may irritate. Dead men cannot feel. You are not dead. If you were, and your life hid in Christ, a thousand things which you now notice, and which afflict you, would be passed by as unworthy of notice, you would then be grasping the eternal and would be above the petty trials of this life.

5T 512   There are three ways in which the Lord reveals His will to us, to guide us, and to fit us to guide others. How may we know His voice from that of a stranger? How shall we distinguish it from the voice of a false shepherd? God reveals His will to us in His word, the Holy Scriptures. His voice is also revealed in His providential workings; and it will be recognized if we do not separate our souls from Him by walking in our own ways, doing according to our own wills, and following the promptings of an unsanctified heart, until the senses have become so confused that eternal things are not discerned, and the voice of Satan is so disguised that it is accepted as the voice of God. Another way in which God's voice is heard is through the appeals of His Holy Spirit, making impressions upon the heart, which will be wrought out in the character.... You should have an earnest desire to be pliable in His hands and to follow withersoever He may lead you.

5T 514 It is for you to yield up your will to the will of Jesus Christ; and as you do this, God will immediately take possession and work in you to will and to do His good pleasure. Your whole nature will then be brought under the control of the Spirit of Christ, and even your thoughts will be subject to Him. You cannot control your impulses, your emotions, as you may desire; but you can control your will, and you can make an entire change in your life. By yielding up your will to Christ, your life will be hid with Christ in God and allied to the power which is above all principalities and powers. You will have strength from God that will hold you fast to His strength; and a new light, even the light of living faith, will be possible to you. But your will must cooperate with God's will.

MH 176 The tempted one needs to understand the true force of the will. This is the governing power in the nature of man—the power of decision, of choice. Everything depends on the right action of the will. Desires for goodness and purity are right, so far as they go; but if we stop here, they avail nothing. Many will go down to ruin while hoping and desiring to overcome their evil propensities. They do not yield the will to God. They do not *choose* to serve Him. God has given us the power of choice; it is ours to exercise. We cannot change our hearts, we cannot control our thoughts, our impulses, our affections. We cannot make ourselves pure, fit for God's service. But we can *choose* to serve God,

43

we can give Him our will; then He will work in us to will and to do according to His good pleasure. Thus our whole nature will be brought under the control of Christ. Through the right exercise of the will, an entire change may be made in the life. By yielding up the will to Christ, we ally ourselves with divine power. We receive strength from above to hold us steadfast. A pure and noble life, a life of victory over appetite and lust, is possible to everyone who will unite his weak, wavering human will to the omnipotent, unwavering will of God.

RH November 2, 1886   If the voice of Jesus is not heeded at once, it becomes confused in the mind with a multitude of voices.

RH March 24, 1896   All heaven is waiting the sinner's cooperation and the only barrier that stands in his way is one which he alone can remove, – his own will. He must submit to the will of God, and through repentance and faith come unto God for salvation. No one will be forced against his will; Christ draws, but never compels.

HP 164   Even the thoughts must be brought into subjection to the will of God, and the feelings under the control of reason and religion. Our imagination was not given us to be allowed to run riot and have its own way, without any effort at restraint and discipline. If the thoughts are wrong, the feelings will be wrong; and the thoughts and feelings combined make up the moral character.

RH September 27, 1906   To every one who surrenders fully to God is given the privilege of living without sin, in obedience to the law of heaven.

1SM 400   They never know what it is to have peace and harmony in the soul; for without entire surrender there is no rest, no joy. Almost Christians, yet not fully Christians, they seem near the kingdom of heaven, but they do not enter therein. Almost but not wholly saved means to be not almost but wholly lost.

6T 92 Satan does not want anyone to see the necessity of an entire surrender to God. When the soul fails to make this surrender, sin is not forsaken; the appetites and passions are striving for the mastery; temptations confuse the conscience, so that true conversion does not take place.

RH November 28, 1899 A partial surrender to truth gives Satan free opportunity to work. Until the soul-temple is fully surrendered to God, it is the stronghold of the enemy.

COL 157 In the whole Satanic force there is not power to overcome one soul who in simple trust casts himself on Christ.

Te 276 There are but two powers that control the minds of men – the power of God and the power of Satan.

Chapter 6
Daily Seeking Christ (Not Once Saved)

Psalm 61:8 So I will sing praise to Your name forever, That I may daily perform my vows.

Luke 9:23-24 Then He said to them all, "If anyone desires to come after Me, let him deny himself, and take up his cross daily, and follow Me. For whoever desires to save his life will lose it, but whoever loses his life for My sake will save it."

1 Corinthians 15:31 I affirm, by the boasting in you which I have in Christ Jesus our Lord, I die daily.

Hebrews 3:12 Beware, brethren, lest there be in any of you an evil heart of unbelief in departing from the living God.

RH March 2, 1897 If we have walked with God in fellowship of the Spirit, it is because we have sought Him daily by faith.

SC 52 Now that you have given yourself to Jesus, do not draw back, do not take yourself away from Him, but day by day say, "I am Christ's. I have given myself to Him;" and ask Him to give you His Spirit and keep you by His grace. As it is by giving yourself to God, and believing in Him, that you become His child, so you are to live in Him.

SC 69 Our growth in grace, our joy, our usefulness, -all depend upon our union with Christ. It is by communion with Him, daily, hourly, – by abiding in Him, – that we are to grow in grace. He is not only the Author, but the Finisher of our faith. It is Christ first, last, and always. He is to be with us, not only at the beginning and the end of our course, but at every step of the way.

RH May 5, 1896 At infinite cost, provision has been made that men shall reach the perfection of Christian character. Those who have been privileged to hear the truth, and have been impressed by the Holy Spirit to receive the Holy Scriptures as the voice of God, have no excuse for becoming dwarfs in the religious life. By exercising the ability which God has given, they are to be daily learning, and daily receiving spiritual fervor and power, which have been provided for every true believer. If we would be growing plants in the Lord's garden, we must have a constant supply of spiritual life and earnestness. Growth will then be seen in the faith and knowledge of our Lord Jesus Christ. There is no half-way house where we may throw off responsibility, and rest by the way. We are to keep advancing heavenward, developing a solid religious character.

1SM 359-360 We are not safe if we neglect to search the Scriptures daily for light and knowledge.... It is to be entertained in the mind, welcomed in the heart, and be cherished, loved, and obeyed.

1SM 374 In order that we may have the righteousness of Christ, we need daily to be transformed by the influence of the Spirit, to be a partaker of the divine nature. It is the work of the Holy Spirit to elevate the taste, to sanctify the heart, to ennoble the whole man.

2SM 380-381 God requires now what He required of Adam, perfect obedience, righteousness without a flaw, without shortcoming in His sight. God help us to render to Him all His law requires. We cannot do this without that faith that brings Christ's righteousness into daily practice.

COL 314 The truth is to be planted in the heart. It is to control the mind and regulate the affections. The whole character must be stamped with the divine utterances. Every jot and tittle of the word of God is to be brought into the daily practice.

Chapter 7
Christ is the Power of Change

Isaiah 45:24 Surely in the Lord I have righteousness and strength.

John 14:5-6 Thomas said to Him, "Lord,... how can we know the way?" Jesus said to him, "I am the way, the truth, and the life. No one comes to the Father except through Me.

John 14:16-17 And I will pray the Father, and He will give you another Helper, that He may abide with you forever, even the Spirit of truth, whom the world cannot receive, because it neither sees Him nor knows Him; but you know Him, for He dwells with you and will be in you.

John 15:4 Abide in Me, and I in you. As the branch cannot bear fruit of itself, unless it abides in the vine, neither can you, unless you abide in Me.

Romans 16:25-26 Now to Him who is able to establish you according to my gospel and the preaching of Jesus Christ, according to the revelation of the mystery kept secret since the world began but now made manifest, and by the prophetic Scriptures made known to all nations, according to the commandment of the everlasting God, for obedience to the faith.

Hebrews 10:16 I will put My laws into their hearts, and in their minds I will write them.

1 Corinthians 1:30 But of Him you are in Christ Jesus, who became for us wisdom from God – and righteousness, and sanctification and redemption – that, as it is written "He who glories, let him glory in the Lord."

1 Corinthians 15:57 But thanks be to God, who gives us the victory through our Lord Jesus Christ.

Galatians 2:20 I have been crucified with Christ; it is no longer I who live, but Christ lives in me; and the life which I now live in the flesh I live by faith in the Son of God, who loved me and gave Himself for me.

Ephesians 2:8-10   For by grace you have been saved through faith, and that not of yourselves; it is the gift of God, not of works, lest anyone should boast. For we are His workmanship, created in Christ Jesus for good works, which God prepared beforehand that we should walk in them.

Colossians 2:9-10   For in Him dwells all the fullness of the Godhead bodily; and you are complete in Him, who is the head of all principality and power.

1 Thessalonians 5:23-24   Now may the God of peace Himself sanctify you completely; and may your whole spirit, soul, and body be preserved blameless at the coming of our Lord Jesus Christ. He who calls you is faithful, who also will do it.

1 Peter 1:5   Who are kept by the power of God through faith for salvation ready to be revealed in the last time.

1 Peter 2:24   Who Himself bore our sins in His own body on the tree, that we, having died to sins, might live for righteousness—by whose stripes you were healed.

2 Peter 1:1-4   To those who have obtained like precious faith with us by the righteousness of our God and Savior Jesus Christ:.... as His divine power has given to us all things that pertain to life and godliness, through the knowledge of Him who called us by glory and virtue, by which have been given to us exceedingly great and precious promises, that through these you may be partakers of the divine nature, having escaped the corruption that is in the world through lust.

Jude 1:1   To those who are called, sanctified by God the Father, and preserved in Jesus Christ.

Philippians 2:13   For it is God who works in you both to will and to do for His good pleasure.

SC 18   There must be a power working from within, a new life from above, before men can be changed from sin to holiness. That power is Christ. His grace alone can quicken the lifeless faculties of the soul, and attract it to God, to holiness.

SC 20 Christ connects fallen man in his weakness and helplessness with the Source of infinite power.

SC 25-26 A repentance such as this, is beyond the reach of our own power to accomplish; it is obtained only from Christ who ascended up on high and has given gifts unto men....Christ is the source of every right impulse. He is the only one that can implant in the heart enmity against sin. Every desire for truth and purity, every conviction of our own sinfulness, is an evidence that His Spirit is moving upon our hearts.

SC 48 By yielding up your will to Christ, you ally yourself with the power that is above all principalities and powers. You will have strength from above to hold you steadfast, and thus through constant surrender to God you will be enabled to live the new life, even the life of faith.

SC 57 That regenerating power, which no human eye can see, begets a new life in the soul; it creates a new being in the image of God.

SC 60 It is faith, and faith only that makes us partakers of the grace of Christ, which enables us to render obedience.

SC 62-63 Because of his [Adam's] sin our natures are fallen and we cannot make ourselves righteous. Since we are sinful, unholy, we cannot perfectly obey the holy law. We have no righteousness of our own with which to meet the claims of the law of God. But Christ has made a way of escape for us.... He lived a sinless life. He died for us and now He offers to take our sins and give us His righteousness. If you give yourself to Him, and accept Him as your Saviour, then sinful as your life may have been, for His sake you are accounted righteous. Christ's character stands in place of your character, and you are accepted before God just as if you had not sinned. More than this, Christ changes the heart. He abides in your heart by faith. You are to maintain this connection with Christ by faith and the continual surrender of your will to Him; and so long as you do this, He will work in you to will and to do according to His good pleasure.

…Then with Christ working in you, you will manifest the same spirit and do the same good works – works of righteousness, obedience. So we have nothing in ourselves of which to boast. We have no ground for self-exaltation. Our only ground of hope is in the righteousness of Christ imputed to us, and in that wrought by His Spirit working in and through us.

SC 69 You are just as dependent upon Christ, in order to live a holy life, as is the branch upon the parent stock for growth and fruitfulness. Apart from Him you have no life. You have no power to resist temptation or to grow in grace and holiness. Abiding in Him, you may flourish. Drawing your life from Him, you will not wither nor be fruitless. You will be like a tree planted by the rivers of water.

SC 70 By faith you became Christ's, and by faith you are to grow up in Him – by giving and taking. You are to give all, -your heart, your will, your service, -give yourself to Him to obey all His requirements; and you must take all, Christ, the fullness of all blessing, to abide in your heart, to be your strength, your righteousness, your everlasting helper, -to give you power to obey.

COL 314 Satan had claimed that it was impossible for man to obey God's commandments; and in our own strength it is true that we cannot obey them. But Christ came in the form of humanity, and by His perfect obedience he proved that humanity and divinity combined can obey every one of God's precepts.

1SM 363-364 Genuine faith appropriates the righteousness of Christ, and the sinner is made an overcomer with Christ; for he is made a partaker of the divine nature, and thus divinity and humanity are combined.

1SM 374 It is the work of the Holy Spirit to elevate the taste, to sanctify the heart, to ennoble the whole man.

1SM 395 Through the work of the Holy Spirit, the sanctification of the truth, the believer becomes fitted for the courts of heaven; for Christ works within us, and His righteousness is upon us. Without this no soul will be entitled to heaven. We would not enjoy heaven unless qualified for its holy atmosphere by the influence of the Spirit and the righteousness of Christ.

2SM 368 In this time of peril we can stand only as we have the truth and the power of God. Men can know the truth only by being themselves partakers of the divine nature.

AA 478 Moral and spiritual perfection, through the grace and power of Christ, is promised to all. Jesus is the source of power, the fountain of life.

DA 161 No man can of himself cast out the evil throng that have taken possession of the heart. Only Christ can cleanse the soul temple. But He will not force an entrance.

RH November 24, 1896 He will quicken your conscience, renew your heart, sanctify your affections, purify your thoughts, and set all your powers at work for Him. Every motive and every thought will be brought into captivity to Jesus Christ.

MH 130 Apart from divine power, no genuine reform can be effected. Human barriers against natural and cultivated tendencies are but as the sandbank against the torrent. Not until the life of Christ becomes a vitalizing power in our lives can we resist the temptations that assail us from within and from without.

Special Testimonies, Series A, 9:62 What is justification by faith? It is the work of God in laying the glory of man in the dust, and doing for man that which is not in his power to do for himself. When men see their own nothingness, they are prepared to be clothed with the righteousness of Christ.

Chapter 8
New Birth Is Immediate Transformation

Isaiah 55:7 Let the wicked forsake his way, and the unrighteous man his thoughts; Let him return to the Lord.

Ezekiel 36:26-27 I will give you a new heart and put a new spirit within you; I will take the heart of stone out of your flesh and give you a heart of flesh. I will put My Spirit within you and cause you to walk in My statutes and you will keep My judgments and do them.

Daniel 4:27 Therefore, O king, let my advice be acceptable to you; break off your sins by being righteous.

Matthew 12:35 A good man out of the good treasure of his heart brings forth good things, and an evil man out of the evil treasure brings forth evil things.

Matthew 18:3-4 Assuredly, I say to you, unless you are converted and become as little children, you will by no means enter the kingdom of heaven. Therefore whoever humbles himself as this little child is the greatest.

John 1:12-13 But as many as received Him, to them He gave the right to become children of God, to those who believe in His name: who were born, not of blood, nor of the will of the flesh, nor of the will of man, but of God.

John 3:3-7 Most assuredly, I say to you, unless one is born again, he cannot see the kingdom of God. Nicodemus said to Him, "How can a man be born when he is old?..." Jesus answered, "Most assuredly I say to you, unless one is born of water and the Spirit, he cannot enter the kingdom of God. That which is born of the flesh is flesh, and that which is born of the Spirit is spirit. Do not marvel that I said to you, 'You must be born again.'"

Acts 2:37-42 Now when they heard this, they were cut to the heart, and said to Peter and the rest of the apostles, "Men and brethren, what shall we do?" Then Peter said to them, "Repent and let every one of you be baptized in the name of Jesus Christ for the remission of sins; and you shall receive the gift of the Holy Spirit. For the promise is to you and to your children and to all who are afar off, as many as the Lord our God will call." And with many other words he testified and exhorted them, saying, "Be saved from this perverse generation." Then those who gladly received his word were baptized; and that day about three thousand souls were added to them. And they continued steadfastly in the apostles' doctrine and fellowship, in the breaking of bread, and in prayers.

Acts 26:18   To open their eyes, in order to turn them from darkness to light, and from the power of Satan to God, that they may receive forgiveness of sins and an inheritance among those who are sanctified by faith in Me.

Romans 6:3-7   Or do you not know that as many of us as were baptized into Christ Jesus were baptized into His death? Therefore we were buried with Him through baptism into death, that just as Christ was raised from the dead by the glory of the Father, even so we also should walk in newness of life. For if we have been united together in the likeness of His death, certainly we also shall be in the likeness of His resurrection, knowing this that our old man was crucified with Him, that the body of sin might be done away with, that we should no longer be slaves of sin. For he who has died has been freed from sin.

Romans 6:11-18   Likewise, you also, reckon yourselves to be dead indeed to sin, but alive to God in Christ Jesus our Lord. Therefore do not let sin reign in your mortal body, that you should obey it in its lusts. And do not present your members as instruments of unrighteousness to sin, but present yourselves to God as being alive from the dead, and your members as instruments of righteousness to God. For sin shall not have dominion over you, for you are not under law but under grace. What then? Shall we sin because we are not under the law but under grace? Certainly not! Do you not know that to whom you present yourselves slaves to obey, you are that one's slaves whom you obey, whether of sin to death, or of obedience to righteousness? But God be thanked that though you were slaves of sin, yet you obeyed from the heart that form of doctrine to which you were delivered. And having been set free from sin, you became slaves of righteousness.

Romans 6:19 I speak in human terms because of the weakness of your flesh. For just as you presented your members as slaves of uncleanness, and of lawlessness leading to more lawlessness, so now present your members as slaves of righteousness for holiness.

Romans 6:22 But now having been set free from sin, and having become slaves of God, you have your fruit to holiness, and the end, everlasting life.

Romans 7:4-6 Therefore, my brethren, you also have become dead to the law through the body of Christ, that you may be married to another – to Him who was raised from the dead, that we should bear fruit to God. For when we were in the flesh, the passions of sin which were aroused by the law were at work in our members to bear fruit to death. But now we have been delivered from the law, having died to what we were held by, so that we should serve in the newness of the Spirit and not in the oldness of the letter.

Romans 8:1-6 There is therefore now no condemnation to those who are in Christ Jesus, who do not walk according to the flesh, but according to the Spirit. For the law of the Spirit of life in Christ Jesus has made me free from the law of sin and death. For what the law could not do in that it was weak through the flesh, God did by sending His own Son in the likeness of sinful flesh, on account of sin: He condemned sin in the flesh, that the righteous requirement of the law might be fulfilled in us who do not walk according to the flesh but according to the Spirit. For those who live according to the flesh set their minds on the things of the flesh, but those who live according to the Spirit, the things of the Spirit. For to be carnally minded is death, but to be spiritually minded is life and peace.

Romans 8:9-10 But you are not in the flesh but in the Spirit, if indeed the Spirit of God dwells in you. Now if anyone does not have the Spirit of Christ, he is not His. And if Christ is in you, the body is dead because of sin, but the Spirit is life because of righteousness.

Romans 8:13-14 For if you live according to the flesh you will die; but if by the Spirit you put to death the deeds of the body, you will live. For as many as are led by the Spirit of God, these are sons of God.

Romans 12:1-2 I beseech you therefore, brethren, by the mercies of God, that you present your bodies a living sacrifice, holy, acceptable to God, which is your reasonable service. And do not be conformed to this world, but be transformed by the renewing of your mind, that you may prove what is the good and acceptable and perfect will of God.

2 Corinthians 5:17 If anyone is in Christ, he is a new creation: old things have passed away; behold, all things have become new.

2 Corinthians 7:1 Therefore, having these promises, beloved, let us cleanse ourselves from all filthiness of the flesh and spirit, perfecting holiness in the fear of God.

Ephesians 2:1-5 And you He made alive, who were dead in trespasses and sins, in which you once walked according to the course of this world, according to the prince of the power of the air, the spirit who now works in the sons of disobedience, among whom also we all once conducted ourselves in the lusts of our flesh, fulfilling the desires of the flesh and of the mind, and were by nature children of wrath, just as the others. But God, who is rich in mercy, because of His great love with which He loved us, even when we were dead in trespasses, made us alive together with Christ.

Ephesians 4:21-24 If indeed you have heard Him and have been taught by Him, as the truth is in Jesus: that you put off, concerning your former conduct, the old man which grows corrupt according to the deceitful lusts, and be renewed in the spirit of your mind, and that you put on the new man which was created according to God, in true righteousness and holiness.

Ephesians 5:8-9 For you were once darkness, but now you are light in the Lord. Walk as children of light (for the fruit of the Spirit is in all goodness, righteousness, and truth).

Philippians 2:15 That you may become blameless and harmless, children of God without fault in the midst of a crooked and perverse generation, among whom you shine as lights in the world.

Titus 2:11-14 For the grace of God that brings salvation has appeared to all men, teaching us that, denying ungodliness and worldly lusts, we should live soberly, righteously, and godly in the present age, looking for the blessed hope and glorious appearing of our great God and Savior Jesus Christ, who gave Himself for us, that He might redeem us from every lawless deed and purify for Himself His own special people, zealous for good works.

1 Thessalonians 4:7 For God did not call us to uncleanness, but in holiness.

1 Peter 1:3-5 Blessed be the God and Father of our Lord Jesus Christ, who according to His abundant mercy has begotten us again to a living hope through the resurrection of Jesus Christ from the dead, to an inheritance incorruptible and undefiled and that does not fade away, reserved in heaven for you, who are kept by the power of God through faith for salvation ready to be revealed in the last time.

1 Peter 1:23 Having been born again, not of corruptible seed but incorruptible, through the word of God which lives and abides forever.

1 Peter 2:24-25 Who Himself bore our sins in His own body on the tree, that we, having died to sins, might live for righteousness – by whose stripes you were healed. For you were like sheep going astray, but have now returned to the Shepherd and Overseer of your souls.

1 Peter 2:7-10   Therefore, to you who believe, He is precious; but to those who are disobedient, "The stone which the builders rejected has become the chief cornerstone,"and "a stone of stumbling and a rock of offense." They stumble, being disobedient to the word, to which they also were appointed.   But you are a chosen generation, a royal priesthood, a holy nation, His own special people, that you may proclaim the praises of Him who called you out of darkness into His marvelous light; who once were not a people but are now the people of God, who had not obtained mercy but now have obtained mercy.

1 John 2:12-14   I write to you, little children, because your sins are forgiven you for His name's sake. I write to you, fathers, because you have known Him who is from the beginning. I write to you, young men, because you have overcome the wicked one.   I write to you, little children, because you have known the Father. I have written to you, fathers, because you have known Him who is from the beginning.   I have written to you, young men, because you are strong, and the word of God abides in you, and you have overcome the wicked one.

4T 17   True conversion is a radical change. The very drift of the mind and bent of the heart should be turned and life become new again in Christ.

AA 284   The life-giving power of the Holy Spirit, proceeding from the Saviour, pervades the soul, renews the motives and affections, and brings even the thoughts into obedience to the will of God, enabling the receiver to bear the precious fruit of holy deeds.

1SM 213   There is no safety or repose nor justification in transgression of the law. Man cannot hope to stand innocent before God, and at peace with Him through the merits of Christ, while he continues in sin.   He must cease to transgress, and become loyal and true.

1SM 327-328   We are to surrender our hearts to God, that He may renew and sanctify us, and fit us for His heavenly court. We are not to wait for some special time, but today we are to give ourselves to Him, refusing to be servants of sin. Do you imagine you can leave off sin a little at a time? Oh, leave the accursed thing at once! Hate the things that Christ hates, love the things that Christ loves. Has He not by His death and suffering made provision for your cleansing from sin? When we begin to realize that we are sinners, and fall on the Rock to be broken, the everlasting arms are placed about us, and we are brought close to the heart of Jesus. Then we shall be charmed with His loveliness, and disgusted with our own righteousness.

RH April 12, 1892 The old nature, born of blood and the will of the flesh, cannot inherit the kingdom of God. The old ways, the hereditary tendencies, the former habits, must be given up; for grace is not inherited. The new birth consists in having new motives, new tastes, new tendencies. Those who are begotten unto a new life by the Holy Spirit have become partakes of the divine nature, and in all their habits and practices they will give evidence of their relationship to Christ. When men who claim to be Christians retain all their natural defects of character and disposition, in what does their position differ from that of the worldling? They do not appreciate the truth as a sanctifier, a refiner. They have not been born again.

GC 468 In the new birth the heart is brought into harmony with God, as it is brought into accord with His law. When this mighty change has taken place in the sinner, he has passed from death unto life, from sin unto holiness, from transgression and rebellion to obedience and loyalty. The old life of alienation and rebellion to obedience and loyalty. The old life of alienation from God has ended; the new life of reconciliation, of faith and love, has begun. Then "the righteousness of the law" will "be fulfilled in us, who walk not after the flesh, but after the Spirit." Rom 8:4

GC 508   In the unregenerate heart there is love of sin and a disposition to cherish and excuse it.   In the renewed heart there is hatred of sin and a determined resistance against it.

DA 311   Christ always separates the contrite soul from sin. He came to destroy the works of the devil, and He has made provision that the Holy Spirit shall be imparted to every repentant soul, to keep him from sinning.

DA 555   No sooner did Zacchaeus yield to the influence of the Holy Spirit than he cast aside every practice contrary to integrity.   No repentance is genuine that does not work reformation.   The righteousness of Christ is not a cloak to cover unconfessed and unforsaken sin; it is a principle of life that transforms the character and controls the conduct. Holiness is wholeness for God; it is the entire surrender of heart and life to the indwelling of the principles of heaven.

SC 57   While the work of the Spirit is silent and imperceptible, its effects are manifest. If the heart has been renewed by the Spirit of God, the life will bear witness to the fact....our lives will reveal whether the grace of God is dwelling within us. A change will be seen in the character, the habits, the pursuits.   The contrast will be clear and decided between what they have been and what they are.

SC 34   Christ is ready to set us free from sin, but He does not force the will.

SC 39   Confession will not be acceptable to God without sincere repentance and reformation.   There must be decided changes in the life; everything offensive to God must be put away.

SC 49   You have confessed your sins, and in heart put them away.   You have resolved to give yourself to God.   Now go to Him, and ask that He will wash away your sins and give you a new heart.   Then believe that He does this because He has promised.

SC 51   You will to serve Him.   Just as surely as you do this, God will fulfill His word to you. If you believe the promise – believe that you are forgiven and cleansed, – God supplies the fact; you are made whole, just as Christ gave the paralytic power to walk when the man believed that he was healed. It is so if you believe it. Do not wait to feel that you are made whole, but say, "I believe it, it is so, not because I feel it, but because God has promised."

SC 52 Through this simple act of believing in God, the Holy Spirit has begotten a new life in your heart.

SC 53 He is waiting to strip them of their garments stained and polluted with sin, and to put upon them the white robes of righteousness; He bids them live and not die.

SC 63-64 Where there is not only a belief in God's word, but a submission of the will to Him; where the heart is yielded to Him, the affections fixed upon Him, there is faith – faith that works by love and purifies the soul. Through this faith the heart is renewed in the image of God. And the heart that in its unrenewed state is not subject to the law of God, neither indeed can be, now delights in its holy precepts, exclaiming with the psalmist, "O how I love Thy law! It is my meditation all the day" Psalm 119:97 And the righteousness of the law is fulfilled in us "Who walk not after the flesh, but after the Spirit." Romans 8:1

SC 67 The change of heart by which we become children of God is in the Bible spoken of as birth.

SC 73 When Christ abides in the heart the whole nature is transformed.

RH May 5, 1896 How the new birth is accomplished matters not, so long as the heart is renewed. When the prayer is sincerely offered, "Create in me a clean heart, O God; and renew a right spirit within me," the voice of the Lord answers, "A new heart also will I give you, and a new spirit will I put within you: and I will take away the stony heart out of your flesh, and I will give you an heart of flesh. And I will put my Spirit within you, and cause you to walk in my statutes, and ye shall keep my judgments and do them." The renewed heart will have no plants of selfishness to cultivate. Pride will be seen in its sinfulness, and will be expelled. It is not for the human clay to find fault with the molding process of the potter, but to submit to be molded in any way. Every soul must submit to the Lord.

9T 188   May the Lord help us to die to self and be born again, that Christ may life in us, a living, active principle, a power that will keep us holy.

MYP 72   To have a new heart is to have a new mind, new purposes, new motives. What is the sign of a new heart? – a changed life.

MS 148, 1897   The new birth is a rare experience in this age of the world. This is the reason why there are so many perplexities in the churches. Many, so many, who assume the name of Christ are unsanctified and unholy. They have been baptized, but they were buried alive. Self did not die, and therefore they did not rise to newness of life in Christ.

RH May 5, 1896   Though we cannot see the Spirit of God, we know that men who have been dead in trespasses and sins, become convicted and converted under its operations. The thoughtless and wayward become serious. The hardened repent of their sins, and the faithless believe…. When we see these changes in the character, we may be assured that the converting power of God has transformed the entire man. We saw not the Holy Spirit, but we saw the evidence of its work on the changed character of those who were hardened and obdurate sinners.

RH November 24, 1896   He will quicken your conscience, renew your heart, sanctify your affections, purify your thoughts, and set all your powers at work for Him. Every motive and every thought will be brought into captivity to Jesus Christ.

DA 172   The Christian's life is not a modification or improvement of the old, but a transformation of nature. There is a death to self and sin, and a new life altogether. This change can be brought about only by the effectual working of the Holy Spirit.

DA 173   When the Spirit of God takes possession of the heart, it transforms the life.   Sinful thoughts are put away, evil deeds are renounced; love, humility, and peace take the place of anger, envy, and strife.   Joy takes the place of sadness, and the countenance reflects the light of heaven.   No one sees the hand that lifts the burden, or beholds the light descend from the courts above.   The blessing comes when by faith the soul surrenders itself to God.   Then that power which no human eye can see creates a new being in the image of God.

DA 280   "The sacrifices of God are a broken spirit: a broken and a contrite heart, O God, Thou wilt not despite."   Psalm 51:17.   Man must be emptied of self before he can be, in the fullest sense, a believer in Jesus.   When self is renounced, then the Lord can make man a new creature…. The love of Christ will animate the believer with new life.   In him who looks unto the Author and Finisher of our faith the character of Christ will be manifest.

COL 163   As the sinner, drawn by the power of Christ, approaches the uplifted cross, and prostrates himself before it, there is a new creation.   A new heart is given him.   He becomes a new creature in Christ Jesus.   Holiness finds that is has nothing more to require.   God Himself is "the justifier of him which believeth in Jesus." Romans 3:26

MYP 69   God has redeemed us from the slavery of sin, and has made it possible for us to live regenerated, transformed lives of service.

TMK 336   The grace of Christ purifies while it pardons, and fits men for a holy heaven.

SD 288   God will not make the slightest compromise with sin.   If he could have done this, Christ need not have come to our world to suffer and die.   No conversion is genuine which does not change both the character and the conduct of those who accept the truth.

Chapter 9
Obey God in Love

Deuteronomy 7:9 Therefore know that the LORD your God, He is God, the faithful God who keeps covenant and mercy for a thousand generations with those who love Him and keep His commandments.

John 14:15 If you love Me, keep My commandments.

John 14:21 He who has My commandments and keeps them, it is he who loves Me. And he who loves Me will be loved by my Father, and I will love him and manifest myself to him.

John 14:23-24 Jesus answered and said to him, "If anyone loves Me, he will keep My word; and My Father will love him, and We will come to him and make Our home with him. He who does not love Me does not keep My words; and the word which you hear is not Mine but the Father's who sent Me.

Ephesians 6:6 Not with eyeservice, as men-pleasers, but as bondservants of Christ, doing the will of God from the heart.

Philippians 2:13 For God is at work in you, both to will and to do for his good pleasure.

1 John 2:5-6 But whoever keeps His word, truly the love of God is perfected in him. By this we know that we are in Him. He who says he abides in Him ought himself also to walk just as He walked.

2 John 1:6 And this is love, that we walk according to His commandments. This is the commandment, just as you have heard from the beginning, that you should walk in it.

1 John 5:3 For this is the love of God, that we keep His commandments. And His commandments are not burdensome.

SC 27 Christ manifested a love that is incomprehensible; and as the sinner beholds this love, it softens the heart, impresses the mind, and inspires contrition of soul.

SC 45 Those who feel the constraining love of God, do not ask how little may be given to meet the requirements of God; they do not ask for the lowest standard, but aim at perfect conformity to the will of their Redeemer. With earnest desire they yield all and manifest an interest proportionate to the value of the object which they seek. A profession of Christ without this deep love is mere talk, dry formality, and heavy drudgery.

SC 58 Who has the heart? With whom are our thoughts? Of whom do we love to converse? Who has our warmest affections and our best energies? If we are Christ's, our thoughts are with Him, and our sweetest thoughts are of Him. All we have and are is consecrated to Him. We long to bear His image, breathe His spirit, do His will, and please Him in all things.

SC 59 In the heart renewed by divine grace, love is the principle of action. It modifies the character, governs the impulses, controls the passions, subdues enmity, and ennobles the affections. This love, cherished in the soul, sweetens the life and sheds a refining influence on all around.

SC 60 Obedience – the service and allegiance of love – is the true sign of discipleship.

MB 76-77 With untold love our God has loved us, and our love awakens toward Him as we comprehend something of the length and breadth and depth and height of his love that passeth knowledge. By the revelation of the attractive loveliness of Christ, by the knowledge of His love expressed to us while we were yet sinners, the stubborn heart is melted and subdued, and the sinner is transformed and becomes a child of heaven. God does not employ compulsory measures; love is the agent which He used to expel sin from the heart. By it He changes pride into humility, and enmity and unbelief into love and faith.

COL 97 The man who attempts to keep the commandments of God from a sense of obligation merely – because he is required to do so – will never enter into the joy of obedience. He does not obey. When the requirements of God are accounted a burden because they cut across human inclination, we may know that the life is not a Christian life. True obedience is the outworking of a principle within. It springs from the love of righteousness, the love of the law of God. The essence of all righteousness is loyalty to our Redeemer.

DA 176 The light shining from the cross reveals the love of God. His love is drawing us to Himself. If we do not resist this drawing, we shall be led to the foot of the cross in repentance for the sins that have crucified the Saviour. Then the Spirit of God through faith produces a new life in the soul. The thoughts and desires are brought into obedience to the will of Christ. The heart, the mind, are created anew in the image of Him who works in us to subdue all things to Himself.

DA 668 All true obedience comes from the heart. It was heart work with Christ. And if we consent, He will so identify Himself with our thoughts and aims, so blend our hearts and minds into conformity to His will, that when obeying Him we shall be but carrying out our own impulses. The will, refined and sanctified, will find its highest delight in doing His service. When we know God as it is our privilege to know Him, our life will be a life of continual obedience.

Chapter 10
Obedience Is Required to Enter Heaven

Psalms 24:3-4 Who may ascend into the hill of the Lord? Or who may stand in His holy place? He who has clean hands and a pure heart, who has not lifted up his soul to an idol, nor sworn deceitfully.

Matthew 5:48 Therefore you shall be perfect, just as your Father in heaven is perfect.

Matthew 7:24 Therefore whoever hears these sayings of Mine, and does them, I will liken him to a wise man who built his house on the rock.

Matthew 19:17 If you want to enter into life, keep the commandments.

John 15:10,14 If you keep My commandments, you will abide in My love, just as I have kept My Father's commandments and abide in His love…. You are my friends if you do whatever I command you.

Romans 2:13 For not the hearers of the law are just in the sight of God, but the doers of the law will be justified.

Romans 3:31 Do we then make void the law through faith? Certainly not! On the contrary, we establish the law.

Romans 6:1-2 What shall we say then? Shall we continue in sin that grace may abound? Certainly not! How shall we who died to sin live any longer in it?

1 Corinthians 3:16-17 Do you not know that you are the temple of God and that the Spirit of God dwells in you? If anyone defiles the temple of God, God will destroy him. For the temple of God is holy, which temple you are.

1 Corinthians 9:25-27 And everyone who competes for the prize is temperate in all things. Now they do it to obtain a perishable crown, but we for an imperishable crown. Therefore I run thus: not with uncertainty. Thus I fight: not as one who beats the air. But I discipline my body and bring it into subjection, lest, when I have preached to others, I myself should become disqualified.

1 Corinthians 15:34   Awake to righteousness, and do not sin; for some do not have the knowledge of God. I speak this to your shame.

Galatians 5:16   Walk in the Spirit, and you shall not fulfill the lust of the flesh.

Galatians 5:22-25   But the fruit of the Spirit is love, joy, peace, longsuffering, kindness, goodness, faithfulness, gentleness, self-control…. And those who are Christ's have crucified the flesh with its passions and desires. If we live in the Spirit, let us also walk in the Spirit.

Ephesians 1:4   Just as He chose us in Him before the foundation of the world, that we should be holy and without blame before Him in love.

Ephesians 5:27   That He might present it to Himself a glorious church, not having spot or wrinkle or any such thing, but that it should be holy and without blemish.

Philippians 1:10-11   That you may approve the things that are excellent, that you may be sincere and without offense till the day of Christ, being filled with the fruits of righteousness which are by Jesus Christ, to the glory and praise of God.

Philippians 2:15   That you may become blameless and harmless, children of God without fault in the midst of a crooked and perverse generation, among whom you shine as lights in the world.

Colossians 4:12   That you may stand perfect and complete in all the will of God.

1 Timothy 6:12-14   Fight the good fight of faith, lay hold on eternal life, to which you were also called and have confessed the good confession in the presence of many witnesses. I urge you in the sight of God who gives life to all things… that you keep this commandment without spot, blameless until our Lord Jesus Christ's appearing.

Hebrews 12:14   Pursue peace with all people, and holiness, without which no one will see the Lord.

1 Peter 1:14-16   As obedient children, not conforming yourselves to the former lusts, as in your ignorance; but as He who calls you is holy, you also be holy in all your conduct, because it is written, "Be holy, for I am holy."

1 John 2:3-6   Now by this we know that we know Him, if we keep His commandments. He who says, "I know Him" and does not keep His commandments, is a liar and the truth is not in Him. But whoever keeps His word, truly the love of God is perfected in him. By this we know that we are in Him. He who says he abides in Him ought himself also to walk just as He walked.

1 John 3:3   Everyone who has this hope in Him purifies himself, just as He is pure.

1 John 3:6-9   Whoever abides in Him does not sin. Whoever sins has neither seen Him nor known Him. Little children, let no one deceive you. He who practices righteousness is righteous, just as He is righteous…. Whoever has been born of God does not sin, for His seed remains in him; and he cannot sin, because he has been born of God.

1 John 3:24   Now he who keeps His commandments abides in Him, and He in him. And by this we know that He abides in us, by the Spirit whom He has given us.

1 John 5:18   We know that whoever is born of God does not sin; but he who has been born of God keeps himself, and the wicked one does not touch him.

2 Peter 3:14   Therefore, beloved, looking forward to these things, be diligent to be found by Him in peace, without spot and blameless.

Revelation 3:21   To him who overcomes I will grant to sit with Me on My throne, as I also overcame and sat down with My Father on His throne.

Revelation 14:12   Here is the patience of the saints; here are those who keep the commandments of God and the faith of Jesus.

Revelation 21:7 He who overcomes shall inherit all things, and I will be his God and he shall be My son.

Revelation 22:14 Blessed are those who do His commandments, that they may have the right to the tree of life, and may enter through the gates into the city.

SC 58 By the faith of the Son of God they will follow in His steps, reflect His character, and purify themselves even as He is pure. The things they once hated they now love, and the things they once loved they hate.

SC 61 We do not earn salvation by our obedience; for salvation is a free gift of God to be received by faith. But obedience is the fruit of faith.... Here is the true test. If we abide in Christ, if the love of God dwells in us, our feelings, our thoughts, our purposes, our actions, will be in harmony with the will of God as expressed in the precepts of His holy law.

AH 16 If you would be a saint in heaven, you must first be a saint on earth. The traits of character you cherish in life will not be changed by death or by resurrection. You will come up from the grave with the same disposition you manifested in your home and in society. Jesus does not change the character at His coming. The work of transformation must be done now. Our daily lives are determining our destiny.

DA 311 Christ always separates the contrite soul from sin. He came to destroy the works of the devil, and He has made provision that the Holy Spirit shall be imparted to every repentant soul, to keep him from sinning.... There is no excuse for sinning. A holy temper, a Christlike life, is accessible to every repenting, believing child of God.... As the Son of man was perfect in His life, so His followers are to be perfect in their life.

COL 283 There are only two classes in the world today, and only two classes will be recognized in the judgement – those who violate God's law and those who obey it. Christ gave the test by which to prove our loyalty or disloyalty. "If ye love me," He says, "Keep My commandments."

COL 330 Moral perfection is required of all. Never should we lower the standard of righteousness in order to accommodate inherited or cultivated tendencies to wrong-doing. We need to understand that imperfection of character is sin. All righteous attributes of character dwell in God as a perfect, harmonious whole, and every one who receives Christ as a personal Savior is privileged to possess these attributes.

Letter 143, November 5, 1900 God demands perfection from every human being. We are to be perfect in this life of humanity, even as God is perfect in His divine character.

1SM 366 In order for man to be justified by faith, faith must reach a point where it will control the affections and impulses of the heart; and it is by obedience that faith itself is made perfect.

1SM 374 Let no one take up with the delusion so pleasant to the natural heart, that God will accept of sincerity, no matter what may be the faith, no matter how imperfect may be the life. God requires of His child perfect obedience.

2SM 380-381 That which God required of Adam before his fall was perfect obedience to His law. God requires now what He required of Adam, perfect obedience, righteousness without a flaw, without shortcoming in His sight. God help us to render to Him all His law requires. We cannot do this without that faith that brings Christ's righteousness into daily practice.

2T 453 God will accept nothing but purity and holiness; one spot, one wrinkle, one defect in the character, will forever debar them from heaven, with all its glories and treasures.

RH Sept 28, 1897 Search the Scriptures, and you will find that not a son or daughter of Adam is elected to be saved in disobedience to God's commandments.

RH April 28, 1891   No one will enter the kingdom of God unless his passions are subdued, unless his will is brought into captivity to the will of Christ.

AA 425   God cannot lower the requirements of His law to meet the standard of wicked men; neither can man in his own power meet the demands of the law. Only by faith in Christ can the sinner be cleansed from guilt and be enabled to render obedience to the law of His maker.

AA 566   He holds up before us the highest ideal, even perfection. He asks us to be absolutely and completely for Him in this world as He is for us in the presence of God.

Chapter 11
Judged By Our Actions That Reveal Our Heart

Psalms 62:12 Also to You, O Lord, belongs mercy; for You render to each one according to his work.

Proverbs 20:11 Even a child is known by his deeds, whether what he does is pure and right.

Jeremiah 17:10 I, the LORD, search the heart, I test the mind, even to give every man according to his ways, according to the fruit of his doings.

Matthew 16:27 For the Son of Man will come in the glory of His Father with His angels, and then He will reward each according to his works.

Luke 6:43-45 For a good tree does not bear bad fruit, nor does a bad tree bear good fruit. For every tree is known by its own fruit…. A good man out of the good treasure of his heart brings forth good; and an evil man out of the evil treasure of his heart brings forth evil.

Romans 2:6-8 Who will render to each one according to his deeds: eternal life to those who by patient continuance in doing good seek for glory, honor, and immortality; but to those who are self-seeking and do not obey the truth, but obey unrighteousness – indignation and wrath.

2 Corinthians 5:10 For we must all appear before the judgment seat of Christ, that each one may receive the things done in the body, according to what he has done, whether good or bad.

James 2:12 So speak and so do as those who will be judged by the law of liberty. [Liberty from sin. Romans 6:18]

Revelation 2:23 All the churches shall know that I am He who searches the minds and hearts. And I will give to each one of you according to your works.

COL 74 Christ Himself will decide who are worthy to dwell with the family of heaven. He will judge every man according to his words and his works. Profession is as nothing in the scale. It is character that decides destiny.

5T 147   The character, the motives, the desires and purposes, are as clear as the light of the sun to the eye of the Omnipotent. But few bear this in mind. The larger class by far do not realize what a fearful account must be rendered at the bar of God by all the transgressors of His law.

1SM 225   When the judgement shall sit, and the books shall be opened, and every man shall be judged according to the things written in the books, then the tables of stone, hidden by God until that day, will be presented before the world as the standard of righteousness. Then men and women will see that the prerequisite of their salvation is obedience to the perfect law of God. None will find excuse for sin. By the righteous principles of that law, men will receive their sentence of life or death.

Chapter 12
Always Growing in Christ - But Not Sinning

Proverbs 4:18-19   The path of the just is like the shining sun, that shines ever brighter unto the perfect day. The way of the wicked is like darkness; they do not know what makes them stumble.

Ephesians 4:13   Till we all come to the unity of the faith and of the knowledge of the Son of God, to a perfect man to the measure of the stature of the fullness of Christ.

Ephesians 5:26-27   That He might sanctify and cleanse her with the washing of water by the word, that He might present her to Himself a glorious church, not having spot or wrinkle or any such thing, but that she should be holy and without blemish.

Hebrews 2:10   For it was fitting for Him, for whom are all things and by whom are all things, in bringing many sons to glory, to make the author of their salvation perfect through sufferings. [Christ never sinned, yet was still made perfect through sufferings]

Hebrews 5:8-9   Though He was a Son, yet he learned obedience by the things which He suffered. And having been perfected, He became the author of eternal salvation to all who obey Him.

2 Peter 3:18   But grow in the grace and knowledge of our Lord and Savior Jesus Christ.

1T 339-340   Jesus, considered as a man, was perfect, yet He grew in grace. "And Jesus increased in wisdom and stature, and in favor with God and man." Even the most perfect Christian may increase continually in the knowledge and love of God.

COL 65   The germination of the seed represents the beginning of spiritual life, and the development of the plant is a beautiful figure of Christian growth. As in nature, so in grace; there can be no life without growth. The plant must either grow or die. As its growth is silent and imperceptible, but continuous, so is the development of the Christian life. At every stage of development our life may be perfect; yet if God's purpose for us is fulfilled, there will be continual advancement. Sanctification is the work of a lifetime. As our opportunities multiply, our experience will enlarge, and our knowledge increase. We shall become strong to bear responsibility, and our maturity will be in proportion to our privileges.

SC 68 In the matchless gift of His Son, God has encircled the whole world with an atmosphere of grace as real as the air which circulates around the globe. All who choose to breath this life-giving atmosphere will live and grow up to the stature of men and women in Christ Jesus. As the flower turns to the sun,.... so should we turn to the Sun of Righteousness that heaven's light may shine upon us, that our character may be developed into the likeness of Christ.

SC 69 Apart from Him you have no life. You have no power to resist temptation or grow in grace and holiness…. Our growth in grace, our joy, our usefulness, -all depend upon our union with Christ. It is by communion with Him, daily, hourly, – by abiding in Him, – that we are to grow in grace. He is not only the Author, but the Finisher of our faith. It is Christ first, and last, and always.

SC 70 By *faith* you became Christ's, and by faith you are to grow in Him – by giving and taking. You are to *give* all, – your heart, your will, your service, – give yourself to Him to obey all His requirements; and you must *take* all, – Christ, the fullness of all blessing, to abide in your heart, to be your strength, your righteousness, your everlasting helper, -to give you power to obey.

SC 109 And to all eternity men may be ever searching, ever learning, and yet never exhaust the treasures of His wisdom, His goodness, and His power.

SC 112 When the people of God are growing in grace, they will be constantly obtaining a clearer understanding of His word. They will discern new light and beauty in its sacred truths.

SC 112-113 By faith we may look to the hereafter and grasp the pledge of God for a growth of intellect, the human faculties uniting with the divine, and every power of the soul being brought into direct contact with the Source of light.

1SM 375 The Spirit of God works in the believer's soul, enabling him to advance from one line of obedience to another, reaching on from strength to greater strength, from grace to grace in Jesus Christ.

1SM 395 In order to be candidates for heaven we must meet the requirement of the law.... We can do this only as we grasp by faith the righteousness of Christ. By beholding Jesus we receive a living, expanding principle in the heart, and the Holy Spirit carries on the work, and the believer advances from grace to grace, from strength to strength, from character to character. He conforms to the image of Christ, until in spiritual growth he attains unto the measure of the full stature in Christ Jesus. Thus Christ makes an end of the curse of sin, and sets the believing soul free from its action and effect.

RH May 5, 1896 At infinite cost, provision has been made that men shall reach the perfection of Christian character. Those who have been privileged to hear the truth, and have been impressed by the Holy Spirit to receive the Holy Scriptures as the voice of God, have no excuse for becoming dwarfs in the religious life. By exercising the ability which God has given, they are to be daily learning, and daily receiving fervor and power, which have been provided for every true believer. If we would be growing plants in the Lord's garden, we must have a constant supply of spiritual life and earnestness. Growth will then be seen in the faith and knowledge of our Lord Jesus Christ.

Chapter 13
Sanctification is Act of Lifetime: Daily Obedience

Joshua 3:5   And Joshua said to the people, "Sanctify yourselves, for tomorrow the LORD will do wonders among you."

2 Chronicles 29:5   Hear me, Levites! Now sanctify yourselves, sanctify the house of the LORD God of your fathers, and carry out the rubbish from the holy place.

John 17:17   Sanctify them by Your truth. Your word is truth.

John 17:19   And for their sakes I sanctify Myself, that they also may be sanctified by the truth.

1 Corinthians 6:9-11   Do you not know that the unrighteous will not inherit the kingdom of God? Do not be deceived.... And such were some of you. But you were washed, you were sanctified, you were justified in the name of the Lord Jesus Christ and in the Spirit of our God.

1 Thessalonians 4:4   That each of you should know how to possess his own vessel in sanctification and honor.

2 Thessalonians 2:13   Because God from the beginning chose you for salvation through sanctification by the Spirit and belief in the truth.

2 Timothy 2:21   Therefore if anyone cleanses himself from the latter, he will be a vessel for honor, sanctified and useful for the Master, prepared for every good work.

Hebrews 10:14   For by one offering He has perfected forever those who are being sanctified.

MLT 248   Genuine sanctification... is nothing less than a daily dying to self and a daily conformity to the will of God.

AA 477   Each day he must renew his consecration, each day do battle with evil. Old habits, hereditary tendencies to wrong, will strive for the mastery, and against these he is to be ever on guard, striving in Christ's strength for victory.

AA 560-561   Sanctification is not the work of a moment, an hour, a day, but of a lifetime. It is not gained by a happy flight of feeling, but is the result of constantly dying to sin, and constantly living for Christ. Wrongs cannot be righted nor reformations wrought in the character by feeble, intermittent efforts. It is only by long, persevering effort, sore discipline, and stern conflict, that we shall overcome. We know not one day how strong will be our conflict the next. So long as Satan reigns, we shall have self to subdue, besetting sins to overcome; so long as life shall last there will be no stopping place, no point which we can reach and say, I have fully attained. Sanctification is the result of lifelong obedience.

COL 65 The germination of the seed represents the beginning of spiritual life, and the development of the plant is a beautiful figure of Christian growth. As in nature, so in grace; there can be no life without growth. The plant must either grow or die. As its growth is silent and imperceptible, but continuous, so is the development of the Christian life. At every stage of development our life may be perfect; yet if God's purpose for us is fulfilled, there will be continual advancement. Sanctification is the work of a lifetime. As our opportunities multiply, our experience will enlarge, and our knowledge increase. We shall become strong to bear responsibility, and our maturity will be in proportion to our privileges.

AA 558-559 John warred earnestly against his faults; but Judas violated his conscience and yielded to temptation, fastening upon himself more securely his habits of evil. The practice of the truths that Christ taught was at variance with his desires and purposes, and he could not bring himself to yield his ideas in order to receive wisdom from heaven. Instead of walking in the light, he chose to walk in darkness…. John and Judas are representatives of those who profess to be Christ's followers…. Each possessed serious defects of character; and each had access to the divine grace that transforms character… One, daily dying to self and overcoming sin, was sanctified through the truth; the other, resisting the transforming power of grace and indulging selfish desires, was brought into bondage to Satan.

5T 47-48 Every Christian must stand on guard continually, watching every avenue of the soul where Satan might find access. He must pray for divine help and at the same time resolutely resist every inclination to sin. By courage, by faith, by persevering toil, he can conquer. But let him remember that to gain the victory Christ must abide in him and he in Christ.... It is only by personal union with Christ, by communion with Him daily, hourly, that we can bear the fruits of the Holy Spirit.

FLB 249 We are to live only one day at a time. We do not have to do the work of a lifetime in a few hours. We need not look into the future with anxiety; for God has made it possible for us to be overcomers every day.

Chapter 14
Conquerors Through Christ in Every Situation

Deuteronomy 29:29   The secret things belong to the Lord our God, but those things which are revealed belong to us and to our children forever, that we may do all the words of this law.

Deuteronomy 31:8   And the LORD, He is the One who goes before you. He will be with you, He will not leave you nor forsake you; do not fear nor be dismayed.

1 Chronicles 28:9   If you seek Him, He will be found by you; but if you forsake Him, He will cast you off forever.

Job 12:13   With Him are wisdom and strength, He has counsel and understanding.

Psalms 37:5   Commit your way to the LORD, trust also in Him, and He shall bring it to pass.

Isaiah 30:21   Your ears shall hear a word behind you, saying, "This is the way, walk in it," whenever you turn to the right hand or whenever you turn to the left.

Isaiah 41:10   Fear not, for I am with you; be not dismayed for I am your God. I will strengthen you, yes, I will help you, I will uphold you with My righteous right hand.

Mark 10:26-27   And they were greatly astonished, saying among themselves, "Who then can be saved?" But looking at them, Jesus said, "With men it is impossible, but not with God; for with God all things are possible."

Luke 10:19   Behold, I give you the authority to trample on serpents and scorpions, and over all the power of the enemy, and nothing shall by any means hurt you.

John 10:3-5   To him the doorkeeper opens, and the sheep hear his voice; and he calls his own sheep by name and leads them out. And when he brings out his own sheep, he goes before them; and the sheep follow him, for they know his voice. Yet they will by no means follow a stranger, but will flee from him, for they do not know the voice of strangers.

John 14:16-17 And He will give you another Helper, that He may abide with you forever, even the Spirit of truth.

John 14:26 But the Helper, the Holy Spirit, whom the Father will send in My name, He will teach you all things, and bring to your remembrance all things that I said to you.

John 16: 13 However, when He, the Spirit of truth, has come, He will guide you into all truth.

Romans 8:37-39 Yet in all these things we are more than conquerors through Him who loved us. For I am persuaded that neither death nor life, nor angels nor principalities, nor power, nor things present nor things to come, nor height nor depth, nor any other created thing, shall be able to separate us from the love of God which is in Christ Jesus our Lord.

Romans 14:4 Indeed, he will be made to stand, for God is able to make him stand.

1 Corinthians 10:13 God is faithful, who will not allow you to be tempted beyond what you are able, but with the temptation will also make the way of escape, that you may be able to bear it.

2 Corinthians 12:9 And He said to me, "My grace is sufficient for you, for My strength is made perfect in weakness." Therefore most gladly I will rather boast in my infirmities, that the power of Christ may rest upon me.

Ephesians 1:17 That the God of our Lord Jesus Christ, the Father of glory, may give to you the spirit of wisdom and revelation in the knowledge of Him.

Philippians 4:13 I can do all things through Christ who strengthens me.

Ephesians 1:3-4 Blessed be the God and Father of our Lord Jesus Christ, who has blessed us with every spiritual blessing in the heavenly places in Christ, just as He chose us in Him before the foundation of the world, that we should be holy and without blame before Him in love.

Ephesians 2:8-10 For by grace you have been saved through faith, and that not of yourselves; it is the gift of God, not of works, lest anyone should boast. For we are His workmanship, created in Christ Jesus for good works, which God prepared beforehand that we should walk in them.

Colossians 4:6 Let your speech always be with grace, seasoned with salt, that you may know how you ought to answer each one.

1 Thessalonians 5:23-24 Now may the God of peace Himself sanctify you completely; and may your whole spirit, soul, and body be preserved blameless at the coming of our Lord Jesus Christ. He who calls you is faithful, who also will do it.

Hebrews 4:15-16 For we do not have a High Priest who cannot sympathize with our weaknesses, but was in all points tempted as we are, yet without sin. Let us therefore come boldly to the throne of grace, that we may obtain mercy and find grace to help in time of need.

Ephesians 6:10-11 Finally, my brethren, be strong in the Lord and in the power of His might. Put on the whole armor of God, that you may be able to stand against the wiles of the devil.

James 1:2-5 My brethren, count it all joy when you fall into various trials, knowing that the testing of your faith produces patience. But let patience have its perfect work, that you may be perfect and complete, lacking nothing. If any of you lacks wisdom, let him ask of God, who gives to all liberally and without reproach, and it will be given to him.

1 Peter 1:5-7 Who are kept by the power of God through faith for salvation ready to be revealed in the last time. In this you greatly rejoice, though now for a little while, if need be, you have been grieved by various trials, that the genuineness of your faith, being much more precious than gold that perishes, though it is tested by fire, may be found to praise, honor, and glory at the revelation of Jesus Christ.

2 Peter 1:1-4 To those who have obtained like precious faith with us by the righteousness of our God and Savior Jesus Christ ....as His divine power has given to us all things that pertain to life and godliness, through the knowledge of

Him who called us by glory and virtue, by which have been given to us exceedingly great and precious promises, that through these you may be partakes of the divine nature, having escaped the corruption that is in the world through lust.

2 Peter 1:10 Therefore, brethren, be even more diligent to make your call and election sure, for if you do these things you will never stumble.

2 Peter 2:9 The Lord knows how to deliver the godly out of temptations.

1 John 2:27-28 But the anointing which you have received from Him abides in you, and you do not need that anyone teach you; but as the same anointing teaches you concerning all things, and is true, and is not a lie, and just as it has taught you, you will abide in Him. And now, little children, abide in Him, that when He appears, we may have confidence and not be ashamed before Him at His coming.

1 John 5:18 We know that whoever is born of God does not sin; but he who has been born of God keeps himself, and the wicked one does not touch him.

Jude 1:24 Now to Him who is able to keep you from stumbling, and to present you faultless before the presence of His glory with exceeding joy.

Letter 143, November 5, 1900 par. 14 When the Father gave His Son to live and die for man, He placed all the treasures of heaven at our disposal. There is no excuse for sin. God has given us all the advantages He possibly could give, that we may have strength to withstand the temptations of the enemy.

1T 158 If the heart is right, your words, your dress, your acts, will all be right.

4T 623 It is Satan's act to tempt you, but your own act to yield. It is not in the power of all the host of Satan to force the tempted to transgress. There is no excuse for sin.

5T 426 Temptation is not sin. Jesus was holy and pure; yet He was tempted in all points as we are, but with a strength and power that man will never be called upon to endure. In His successful resistance He has left us a bright example, that we should follow in His steps. If we are self-confident or self-righteous we shall be left to fall under the power of temptation; but if we look to Jesus and trust in Him we call to our aid a power that has conquered the foe on the field of battle, and with every temptation He will make a way of escape. When Satan comes in like a flood, we must meet his temptations with the sword of the Spirit, and Jesus will be our helper and will lift up for us a standard against him.

5T 514 You will have strength from God that will hold you fast to His strength; and a new light, even the light of living faith, will be possible to you.

1SM 82 Through the plan of redemption, God has provided means for subduing every sinful trait, and resisting every temptation, however strong.

1SM 363-364 Genuine faith appropriates the righteousness of Christ, and the sinner is made an overcomer with Christ; for he is made a partaker of the divine nature, and thus divinity and humanity are combined.

1SM 364 Looking unto Jesus, the author and finisher of our faith, we may go on from strength to strength, from victory to victory; for through Christ the grace of God has worked out our complete salvation.

1SM 394 Abundant grace has been provided that the believing soul may be kept free from sin; for all heaven, with its limitless resources, has been placed at our command. We are to draw from the well of salvation.

2SM 352-353 The enemy is a master worker, and if God's people are not constantly led by the Spirit of God, they will be snared and taken. By his subtle workings in these last days, he is linking the human mind with his own, imbuing it with the thoughts; and he is doing this work in so deceptive a manner that those who accept his guidance know not that they are being led by him at his will.

2SM 368 In this time of peril we can stand only as we have the truth and the power of God. Men can know the truth only by being themselves partakers of the divine nature.

2SM 368-369 But when the world makes void the law of God, what will be the effect upon the truly obedient and righteous? Will they be carried away by the strong current of evil? Never! Not one who is abiding in Christ will fail or fall.... We are not left to our own direction. In all our ways we should acknowledge God, and He will direct our paths. We should consult His Word with humble hearts, ask his counsel, and give up our will to His. We can do nothing without God.

2SM 370 The prospect of being brought into personal danger and distress, need not cause despondency, but should quicken the vigor and hopes of God's people; for the time of their peril is the season for God to grant them clearer manifestation of His power.

GC 510 The tempter has no power to control the will or to force the soul to sin.

DA 490-491 The Saviour is by the side of His tempted and tried ones. With Him there can be no such thing as failure, loss, impossibility, or defeat; we can do all things through Him who strengthens us. When temptations and trials come, do not wait to adjust all the difficulties, but look to Jesus, your helper.

DA 668 Those who decide to do nothing in any line that will displease God, will know, after presenting their case before Him, just what course to pursue. And they will receive not only wisdom, but strength. Power for obedience, for service, will be imparted to them, as Christ has promised.

GC 530 Satan is well aware that the weakest soul who abides in Christ is more than a match for the hosts of darkness, and that, should he reveal himself openly, he would be met and resisted.

OHC 323 Our heavenly Father measures and weighs every trial before He permits it to come upon the believer. He considers the circumstances and the strength of the one who is to stand under the proving and test of God, and He never permits the temptations to be greater than the capacity of resistance.

PP 421   The strongest temptation cannot excuse sin. However great the pressure brought to bear upon the soul, transgression is our own act. It is not in the power of earth or hell to compel anyone to do evil. Satan attacks us at our weak points, but we need not be overcome. However severe or unexpected the assault, God has provided help for us, and in His strength we may conquer.

FW 49-50   There is no excuse for sin or for indolence. Jesus has led the way, and He wishes us to follow in His steps. He has suffered, He has sacrificed as none of us can, that He might bring salvation within our reach. We need not be discouraged. Jesus came to our world to bring divine power to man, that through His grace, we might be transformed into His likeness. When it is in the heart to obey God, when efforts are put forth to this end, Jesus accepts this disposition and effort as man's best service, and He makes up for the deficiency with His own divine merit. But he will not accept those who claim to have faith in Him and yet are disloyal to His Father's commandment. We hear a great deal about faith, but we need to hear a great deal more about works. Many are deceiving their own souls by living an easy-going, accommodating, crossless religion.

SD 13   Christ loves His church. He will give all needed help to those who call upon Him for strength for the development of Christlike character. But his love is not weakness. He will not serve with their sins or give them prosperity while they continue to follow a wrong course of action. Only by faithful repentance will their sins be forgiven; for God will not cover evil with the robe of His righteousness.

Chapter 15
Three Angels Message: Obey in Faith

Revelation 14:7 Fear God and give glory to Him, for the hour of His judgement has come; and worship Him who made heaven and earth, the sea and springs of water.

Revelation 14:8 Babylon is fallen, is fallen, that great city, because she has made all nations drink of the wine of the wrath of her fornication.

Revelation 14:9-12 Then a third angel followed them, saying with a loud voice, "If anyone worships the beast and his image, and receives his mark on his forehead or on his hand, he himself shall also drink of the wine of the wrath of God, which is poured out full strength into the cup of His indignation. He shall be tormented with fire and brimstone in the presence of the holy angels and in the presence of the Lamb. And the smoke of their torment ascends forever and ever; and they have no rest day or night, who worship the beast and his image, and whoever receives the mark of his name." Here is the patience of the saints; here are those who keep the commandments of God and the faith of Jesus.

TM 91-92 The Lord in His great mercy sent a most precious message to His people through Elders Waggoner and Jones. This message was to bring more prominently before the world the uplifted Saviour, the sacrifice for the sins of the whole world. It presented justification through faith in the Surety; it invited the people to receive the righteousness of Christ, which is made manifest in obedience to all the commandments of God. Many had lost sight of Jesus. They needed to have their eyes directed to His divine person, His merits, and His changeless love for the human family. All power is given into His hands, that He may dispense rich gifts unto men, imparting the priceless gift of His own righteousness to the helpless human agent. This is the message that God commanded to be given to the world. It is the third angel's message, which is to be proclaimed with a loud voice, and attended with the outpouring of His Spirit in a large measure.

RH April 1, 1890 Several have written to me, inquiring if the message of justification by faith is the third angel's message, and I have answered, "It is the third angel's message in verity." The prophet declares, "And after these things I saw another angel come down from heaven, having great power; and the earth was lightened with his glory." Brightness, glory, and power are to be connected with the third angel's message, and conviction will follow wherever it is preached in demonstration of the Spirit.... God has light for his people, and all who will accept it will see the sinfulness of remaining in a lukewarm condition; they will heed the counsel of the True Witness when he says, "Be zealous therefore, and repent. Behold, I stand at the door, and knock: if any man hear my voice, and open the door, I will come in to him, and will sup with him, and he with me.

2SM 402-403 Recently in the night season, my mind was impressed by the Holy Spirit with the thought that if the Lord is coming as soon as we believe He is, we ought to be even more active than we have been in years past in getting the truth before the people. In this connection my mind reverted to the activity of the Advent believers in 1843 and 1844. At that time there was much house-to-house visitation, and untiring efforts were made to warn the people of the things that are spoken of in God's Word. We should be putting forth even greater effort than was put forth by those who proclaimed the first angel's message so faithfully. We are rapidly approaching the end of this earth's history; and as we realize that Jesus is indeed coming soon, we shall be aroused to labor as never before. We are bidden to sound the alarm to the people. And in our own lives we are to show forth the power of truth and righteousness. The world is soon to meet the great Lawgiver over His broken law. Those only who turn from transgression to obedience can hope for pardon and peace. We are to raise the banner on which is inscribed,

"The commandments of God, and the faith of Jesus." Obedience to God's law is the great issue. Let it not be put out of sight. We must strive to arouse church members, and those who make no profession, to see and obey the claims of the law of Heaven. We are to magnify this law and make it honorable.

Chapter 16
Christ in the Home

Proverbs 15:1 A soft answer turns away wrath, but a harsh word stirs up anger.

Proverbs 22:6 Train up a child in the way he should go, and when he is old he will not depart from it.

Proverbs 29:15 The rod and rebuke give wisdom, but a child left to himself brings shame to his mother.

Proverbs 29:17 Correct your son, and he will give you rest; yes, he will give delight to your soul.

Isaiah 49:24-25 Shall the prey be taken from the mighty, or the captives of the righteous be delivered? But thus says the LORD: "Even the captives of the mighty shall be taken away, and the prey of the terrible be delivered; for I will contend with him who contends with you, and I will save your children.

Isaiah 54:13 All your children shall be taught by the LORD, and great shall be the peace of your children.

Jeremiah 31:16-17 Thus says the LORD: "Refrain your voice from weeping, and your eyes from tears; for your work shall be rewarded, says the LORD, and they shall come back from the land of the enemy. There is hope in your future, says the LORD, that your children shall come back to their own border.

Malachi 4:5-6 Behold, I will send you Elijah the prophet before the coming of the great and dreadful day of the LORD. And he will turn the hearts of the fathers to the children, and the hearts of the children to their fathers, lest I come and strike the earth with a curse.

Matthew 12:25 Every city or house divided against itself will not stand.

Matthew 18:10 Take heed that you do not despise one of these little ones, for I say to you that in heaven their angels always see the face of My Father who is in heaven.

1 Corinthians 13:1-7   Though I speak with the tongues of men and of angels, but have not love, I have become sounding brass or a clanging cymbal. And though I have the gift of prophecy, and understand all mysteries and all knowledge, and though I have all faith, so that I could remove mountains, but have not love, I am nothing. And though I bestow all my goods to feed the poor, and though I give my body to be burned, but have not love, it profits me nothing. Love suffers long and is kind; love does not envy; love does not parade itself, is not puffed up; does not behave rudely, does not seek its own, is not provoked, thinks no evil; does not rejoice in iniquity, but rejoices in the truth; bears all things, believes all things, hopes all things, endures all things.

Colossians 4:6   Let your speech always be with grace, seasoned with salt, that you may know how you ought to answer each one.

Ephesians 4:29   Let no corrupt word proceed out of your mouth, but what is good for necessary edification, that it may impart grace to the hearers.

Ephesians 4:31-32   Let all bitterness, wrath, anger, clamor, and evil speaking be put away from you, with all malice. And be kind to one another, tenderhearted, forgiving one another, even as God in Christ forgave you.

Hebrews 12:14-15   Pursue peace with all people, and holiness, without which no one will see the Lord. Looking carefully lest anyone fall short of the grace of God; lest any root of bitterness springing up cause trouble, and by this many become defiled.

James 1:19   So then, my beloved brethren, let every man be swift to hear, slow to speak, slow to wrath.

1 Peter 3:8   Finally, all of you be of one mind, having compassion for one another; love as brothers, be tenderhearted, be courteous.

AH 16   If you would be a saint in heaven, you must first be a saint on earth. The traits of character you cherish in life will not be changed by death or by resurrection. You will come up from the grave with the same disposition you manifested in your home and in society. Jesus does not change the character at His coming. The work of transformation must be done now. Our daily lives are determining our destiny.

MB 16 It is the love of self that destroys our peace. While self is all alive, we stand ready continually to guard it from mortification and insult; but when we are dead, and our life is hid with Christ in God, we shall not take neglects or slights to heart. We shall be deaf to reproach and blind to scorn and insult.

MS 34, 1899 Men and women, children and youth, are measured in the scales of heaven in accordance with that which they reveal in their home life. A Christian in the home is a Christian anywhere.

CG 481 The measure of your Christianity is gauged by the character of your home life. The grace of Christ enables its possessors to make the home a happy place, full of peace and rest. Unless you have the Spirit of Christ, you are none of His.

RH July 12, 1887 But you will say, How am I to know that Christ is in my heart? If when you are criticised or corrected in your way, and things do not go just as you think they ought to go, – if then you let your passion arise instead of bearing the correction and being patient and kind, Christ is not abiding in the heart.

AH 32 One well-ordered family, well-disciplined family tells more in behalf of Christianity than all the sermons that can be preached.

RH March 29, 1892 "O," you may say, "I do keep the commandments." Do you?... Do you carry out the principles of God's commandments in your home, in your family? Do you never manifest rudeness, unkindness, and impoliteness in the family circle? If you do manifest unkindness at your home, no matter how high may be your profession, you are breaking God's commandments. No matter how much you may preach the commandments to others, if you fail to manifest the love of Christ to others in your home life, you are a transgressor of the law.

ML 334   Those who open their hearts and homes to invite Jesus to abide with them should keep the moral atmosphere unclouded by strife, bitterness, wrath, malice, or even an unkind word.   Jesus will not abide in a home where are contention, envy, and bitterness.

HP 99   Words spoken in our homes which are impatient and unkind, angels hear; and do you want to find in the books of heaven a record of the impatient and passionate words you have uttered in your family?   Impatience brings the enemy of God and man into your family and drives out the angels of God.   If you are abiding in Christ, and Christ in you, you cannot speak angry words.

RH July 15, 1902   Prepare for the coming of the Lord.   This is the preparation day.   Set your own hearts in order, and work earnestly for your children.   An unreserved surrender to God will sweep away the barriers that have so long defied the approaches of heavenly grace.   When you take up the cross and follow Christ, when you bring your lives into conformity to the will of God, your children will be converted.

CG 172   If parents would see a different state of things in their family, let them consecrate themselves wholly to God, and the Lord will devise ways and means whereby a transformation may take place in their households.

RH March 28, 1893   Children are the lawful prey of the enemy, because they are not subjects of grace, have not experienced the cleansing power of Jesus, and the evil angels have access to these children; and some parents are careless and suffer them to work with but little restraint. Parents have a great work to do in this matter, by correcting and subduing their children, and then bringing them to God and claiming His blessing upon them.   By the faithful and untiring efforts of the parents, and the blessing and grace entreated of God upon the children, the power of the evil angels will be broken, a sanctifying influence is shed upon the children, and the powers of darkness must give back.

7T 10 On fathers and mothers, God has placed the responsibility of saving their children from the power of the enemy. This is their work, a work that they should on no account neglect. Those parents who have a living connection with Christ will not rest until they see their children safe in the fold. They will make this the burden of their life.

DA 512 Let mothers come to Jesus with their perplexities. They will find grace sufficient to aid them in the management of their children. The gates are open for every mother who would lay her burdens at the Saviour's feet. He who said, "Suffer the little children to come unto Me, and forbid them not," still invites the mothers to lead up their little ones to be blessed by Him. Even the babe in its mother's arms may dwell as under the shadow of the Almighty through the faith of the praying mother. John the Baptist was filled with the Holy Spirit from his birth. If we will live in communion with God, we too may expect the divine Spirit to mold our little ones, even from their earliest moments.

1T 397-398 Come in humility with a heart full of tenderness and with a sense of the temptations and dangers before yourselves and your children; by faith bind them upon the altar, entreating for them the care of the Lord. Ministering angels will guard children who are thus dedicated to God. It is the duty of Christian parents, morning and evening, by earnest prayer and persevering faith, to make a hedge about their children. They should patiently instruct them, kindly and untiringly teach them how to live in order to please God.

5T 322 His "hand is not shortened, that it cannot save; neither his ear heavy, that it cannot hear;" and if Christian parents seek Him earnestly, He will fill their mouths with arguments, and for His name's sake will work mightily in their behalf in the conversion of their children.

CG 557-558   If you have failed in your duty to your families, confess your sins before God. Gather your children about you and acknowledge your neglect. Tell them that you desire to bring about a reformation in the home, and ask them to help you to make the home what it ought to be. Read to them the directions found in the Word of God. Pray with them; and ask God to spare their lives, and to help them to prepare for a home in His kingdom. In this way you may begin a work a reformation; and then continue to keep the way of the Lord.

5T 40   Deal honestly and faithfully with your children. Work bravely and patiently. Fear no crosses, spare no time or labor, burden or suffering. The future of your children will testify the character of your work. Fidelity to Christ on your part can be better expressed in the symmetrical character of your children than in any other way.

RH July 8, 1902   Let parents live in the home the life of Christ, and the transformation in the lives of their children will testify to God's miracle-working power.

CG 286-287   The father, as priest of the household, should deal gently and patiently with his children. He should be careful not to arouse in them a combative disposition. He must not allow transgression to go uncorrected, and yet there is a way to correct without stirring up the worst passions in the human heart. Let him in love talk with his children, telling them how grieved the Saviour is over their course; and then let him kneel with them before the mercy seat and present them to Christ... and ask forgiveness. Such disciplining will nearly always break the most stubborn heart.

CG 219   Let not one word of fretfulness, harshness, or passion escape your lips. The grace of Christ awaits your demand. His Spirit will take control of your heart and conscience, presiding over your words and deeds. Never forfeit your self-respect by hasty, thoughtless words. See that your words are pure, your conversation holy. Give your children an example of that which you wish them to be.

RH June 23, 1903 We have much to learn in regard to child training. When teaching the little ones to do things, we must not scold them. Never should we say, "Why did you not do this?" Say, "Children, help mother do this;" or "Come, children, let us do this." Be their companion in doing these things. When they finish their work, praise them.

ML 173 An approving glance, a word of encouragement or commendation, will be like sunshine in their hearts.

MH 391 The father should enforce in his family the sterner virtues – energy, integrity, honesty, patience, courage, diligence, and practical usefulness. And what he requires of his children he himself should practice, illustrating these virtues in his own manly bearing. But, fathers, do not discourage your children. Combine affection with authority, kindness and sympathy with firm restraint.

2SM 236 When we give way to impatience, we drive the Spirit of God out of the heart, and give place to the attributes of Satan.

TDG 357 When Christ dwells in the heart, His presence is apparent. Good and pleasant words and actions reveal the Spirit of Christ. Sweetness of temper is manifested. There is no angry passion, no obstinacy, no evil-surmising. There is no hatred in the heart.

TMK 167 Do not give the lie to your profession of faith by impatience, fretfulness, and repining. Let the graces of the Spirit be manifested in kindness, meekness, forbearance, cheerfulness, and love. Let it be seen that the love of Christ is an abiding motive; that your religion is not a dress to be put off and on to suit circumstances, but a principle – calm, steady, unwavering.

ED 287 The object of discipline is the training of the child for self-government. He should be taught self-reliance and self-control. Therefore as soon as he is capable of understanding, his reason should be enlisted on the side of obedience. Let all dealing with him be such as to show obedience to be just and reasonable. Help him to see that all things are under law, and that disobedience leads, in the end, to disaster and suffering.

ML 261 Unless parents shall make it the first business of their lives to guide their children's feet into the path of righteousness from their earliest years, the wrong path will be chosen before the right.

SD 130 The earlier the will is made to yield to the will of the parents and the more complete the submission, the less difficult it will be to yield to the requirements of God.

CG 194 Mothers, be sure that you properly discipline your children during the first three years of their lives. Do not allow them to form their wishes and desires. The mother must be mind for her child. The first three years is the time in which to bend the tiny twig. Mothers should understand the importance attaching to this period. It is then that the foundation is laid. If these first lessons have been defective, as they very often are, for Christ's sake, for the sake of your children's future and eternal good, seek to repair the wrong you have done. If you have waited until your children were three years old to begin to teach them self-control and obedience, seek to do it now, even though it will be much harder.

RH March 28, 1893 Many parents will have to render an awful account at last for their neglect of their children. They have fostered and cherished their evil tempers by bending to their wishes and will, when the wishes and will of the children should bend to them. They have brought God's frown upon them and their children by these things.

RH March 28, 1893 You should correct your children in love. Do not let them have their own way until you get angry, and then punish them. Such correction only helps on the evil, instead of remedying it. After you have done your duty faithfully to your children, then carry them to God, and ask Him to help you. Tell Him that you have done your part, and then in faith ask God to do His part, that which you cannot do. Ask Him to temper their dispositions, to make them mild and gentle by His Holy Spirit. He will hear you pray. He will love to answer your prayers.

CG 85 Children should be brought to the point of submission and obedience. Disobedience must not be allowed. Sin lies at the door of the parents who allow their children to disobey.

CG 253 I never allowed my children to think that they could plague me in their childhood. I also brought up in my family others from other families, but I never allowed those children to think that they could plague their mother. Never did I allow myself to say a harsh word or to become impatient or fretful over the children. They never got the better of me once – not once, to provoke me to anger. When my spirit was stirred, or when I felt anything like being provoked, I would say, "Children, we shall let this rest now; we shall not say anything more about it now. Before we retire, we shall talk it over." Having all this time to reflect, by evening they had cooled off, and I could handle them very nicely.... There is a right way, and there is a wrong way. I never lifted a hand to my children, before I talked with them; and if they broke down, and if they saw their mistake (and they always did when I brought it before them and prayed with them), and if they were subdued (and they always were when I did this), then I had them under my control. I never found them otherwise. When I prayed with them, they would break all to pieces, and they would throw their arms around my neck and cry.

3T 532 Children have sensitive, loving natures. They are easily pleased and easily made unhappy. By gently discipline, in loving words and acts, mothers may bind their children to their hearts. To manifest severity and to be exacting with children are great mistakes. Uniform firmness and unimpassioned control are necessary to the discipline of every family. Say what you mean calmly, move with consideration and carry out what you say without deviation. **1T 216-217** Some parents are in subjection to their children. They fear to cross the will of their children, and therefore yield to them. But just as long as children are under the roof of their parents, dependent upon them, they should be subject to their control. Parents should move with decision, requiring their views of right to be followed out.

CG 262 Let them mingle kindness and affection and love with their family government, and yet let them be as firm as a rock to right principles.

PP 579 There is no greater curse upon households than to allow the youth to have their own way. When parents regard every wish of their children and indulge them in what they know is not for their good, the children soon lose all respect for their parents, all regard for the authority of God or man, and are led captive at the will of Satan.

4T 651 Eli was cursed of God because he did not promptly and decidedly restrain his wicked sons.

CG 182 The Lord will not vindicate the misrule of parents. Today hundreds of children swell the ranks of the enemy, living and working apart from the purpose of God. They are disobedient, unthankful, unholy; but the sin lies at the door of their parents. Christian parents, thousands of children are perishing in their sins because of the failure of their parents to rule the home wisely.

RH March 30, 1897 Not a particular of variance should be shown by parents in the management of their children. Parents are to work together as a unit. There must be no division. But many parents work at cross-purposes, and thus the children are spoiled by mismanagement. If parents do not agree, let them absent themselves from the presence of their children until an understanding can be arrived at.

RH July 28, 1910 If you lose your temper, you forfeit that which no mother or father can afford to lose – the respect of your children. Never scold, nor permit scolding, in the home. Never give your child a passionate blow, unless you wish him to learn to quarrel and fight. As parents, you stand in the place of God to your children, and you are to be on guard. Parents, never act from impulse. Never correct your child when you are angry; for if you do this, you will mold him after your image – to be impulsive, passionate, and unreasonable. You can be firm without violent threatenings or scoldings.

CG 525 We should pray to God much more than we do. There is great strength and blessing in praying together in our families, with and for our children.

CG 248 When children have done wrong, they themselves are convicted of their sin and feel humiliated and distressed. To scold them for their faults will often result in making them stubborn and secretive.

CG 244 Exact obedience in your family; but while you do this, seek the Lord with your children, and ask Him to come in and rule.

CG 245 However provoking your children may be in their ignorance, do not give way to impatience. Teach them patiently and lovingly. Be firm with them. Do not let Satan control them. Discipline them only when you are under the discipline of God. Christ will be the victor in the lives of your children if you will learn of Him who is meek and lowly, pure and undefiled.

CG 217 Fathers and mothers, when you can control yourselves, you will gain great victories in controlling your children.

MH 352 Parents may lay for their children the foundation for a healthy, happy life. They may send them forth from their homes with moral stamina to resist temptation, and courage and strength to wrestle successfully with life's problems. They may inspire in them the purpose and develop the power to make their lives an honor to God and a blessing to the world. They may make straight paths for their feet, through sunshine and shadow, to the glorious heights above.

CT 131 This is your day of trust, your day of responsibility and opportunity. Soon will come your day of reckoning. Take up your work with earnest prayer and faithful endeavor. Teach your children that it is their privilege to receive every day the baptism of the Holy Spirit. Let Christ find you His helping hand to carry out His purposes. By prayer you may gain an experience that will make your ministry for your children a perfect success.

SD 132 If the youth would become strong in mind, pure in morals, firm in spiritual power, let them follow the example of Jesus in His simplicity, in His submission to parental restraint.

Chapter 17
False Christianity

Proverbs 14:12   There is a way that seems right to a man, but its end is the way of death.

Matthew 7:21-23   Not everyone who says to Me, "Lord, Lord" shall enter the kingdom of heaven, but he who does the will of My Father in heaven. Many will say to Me in that day, "Lord, Lord, have we not prophesied in Your name, cast out demons in Your name, and done many wonders in Your name?" And then I will declare to them, "I never knew you; depart from Me, you who practice lawlessness!"

Luke 13:23-24   Then one said to Him, "Lord, are there few who are saved?" And He said to them, "Strive to enter through the narrow gate, for many, I say to you, will seek to enter and will not be able."

John 5:39-40   You search the Scriptures, for in them you think you have eternal life; and these are they which testify of Me. But you are not willing to come to Me that you may have life.

Acts 20:29-30   For I know this, that after my departure savage wolves will come in among you, not sparing the flock. Also from among yourselves men will rise up, speaking perverse things, to draw away the disciples after themselves.

2 Corinthians 11:13-15   For such are false apostles, deceitful workers, transforming themselves into apostles of Christ. And no wonder! For Satan himself transforms himself into an angel of light. Therefore it is no great thing if his ministers also transform themselves into ministers of righteousness, whose end will be according to their works.

2 Timothy 4:3-4   For the time will come when they will not endure sound doctrine, but according to their own desires, because they have itching ears, they will heap up for themselves teachers; and they will turn their ears away from the truth, and be turned aside to fables.

Titus 1:16 They profess to know God, but in works they deny Him, being abominable, disobedient, and disqualified for every good work.

1 John 2:4 He who says "I know Him", and does not keep His commandments, is a liar and the truth is not in Him.

1 John 2:15-16 Do not love the world or the things in the world. If anyone loves the world, the love of the Father is not in him. For all that is in the world – the lust of the flesh, the lust of the eyes, and the pride of life – is not of the Father but is of the world.

SC 58 There may be an outward correctness of deportment without the renewing power of Christ. The love of influence and the desire for the esteem of others may produce a well-ordered life. Self-respect may lead us to avoid the appearance of evil. A selfish heart may perform generous actions.

SC 59-60 There are two errors against which the children of God.... especially need to guard. The first.... is that of looking to their own works, trusting to anything they can do, to bring themselves into harmony with God.... The opposite and no less dangerous error is that belief in Christ releases men from keeping the law of God; that since by faith alone we become partakers of the grace of Christ, our works have nothing to do with our redemption.

SC 61 That so-called faith in Christ which professes to release men from the obligation of obedience to God, is not faith, but presumption.

DA 439 Our Lord is put to shame by those who claim to serve Him, but who misrepresent His character; and multitudes are deceived, and led into false paths.

COL 279 In profession they claim to be sons of God, but in life and character they deny the relationship. They do not surrender the will to God. They are living a lie.

5T 477 Do not forget that the most dangerous snares which Satan has prepared for the church will come through its own members.

GC 524   If men would but study the Book of God with earnest prayer that they might understand it, they would not be left in darkness to receive false doctrines. But as they reject the truth they fall prey to deception.

GC 595   The multitudes do not want Bible truth, because it interferes with the desires of the sinful, world-loving heart; and Satan supplies the deceptions which they love…. He leads the people to look to bishops, to pastors, to professors of theology as their guides, instead of searching the Scriptures to learn their duty for themselves. Then, by controlling the minds of these leaders, he can influence the multitudes according to his will.

DA 310   Men may profess faith in the truth; but if it does not make them sincere, kind, patient, forbearing, heavenly-minded, it is a curse to its possessors, and through their influence it is a curse to the world.

RH November 18, 1890   They talk of God's love, claiming that He is not severe and exacting, but long-suffering and lenient; at the same time, they echo the suggestion of Satan,… "Ye shall not surely die."

HP 318   Christ will have nothing to do with pretense. He will welcome to the heavenly courts those only whose Christianity is genuine. The lives of professed Christians who do not live the life of Christ are a mockery to religion.

ML 257   When persons profess to be Christian, and their religion does not make them better men and better women in all the relations of life – living representatives of Christ in disposition and character – they are none of His.

DA 357   A spirit contrary to the spirit of Christ would deny Him, whatever the profession. Men may deny Christ by evil speaking, by foolish talking, by words that are untruthful or unkind. They may deny Him by shunning life's burdens, by the pursuit of sinful pleasures. They may deny Him by conforming to the world, by uncourteous behavior, by the love of their own opinions, by justifying self, by cherishing doubt, borrowing trouble, and dwelling in darkness. In all these ways they declare that Christ is not in them.

MB 150 Not those whose hearts are touched by the Spirit, not those who now and then yield to its power, but they that are led by the Spirit, are the sons of God.

MB 137 It is because men take upon themselves the name of Christ, while in life they deny His character, that Christianity has so little power in the world. The name of the Lord is blasphemed because of these things.

Chapter 18
Definition of Sin

Romans 14:23 Whatever is not from faith is sin.

1 John 3:4 Whoever commits sin also commits lawlessness, and sin is lawlessness.

1 John 5:17 All unrighteousness is sin.

James 1:14-15 But each one is tempted when he is drawn away by his own desires and enticed. Then, when desire has conceived, it gives birth to sin; and sin, when it is full-grown, brings forth death.

James 4:17 To him who knows to do good and does not do it, to him it is sin.

GC 492 It is impossible to explain the origin of sin so as to give a reason for its existence. Yet enough may be understood concerning both the origin and the final disposition of sin to make fully manifest the justice and benevolence of God in all His dealings with evil. Nothing is more plainly taught in Scripture than that God was in no wise responsible for the entrance of sin; that there was no arbitrary withdrawal of divine grace, no deficiency in the divine government, that gave occasion for the uprising of rebellion. Sin is an intruder, for whose presence no reason can be given. It is mysterious, unaccountable; to excuse it is to defend it. Could excuse for it be found, or cause be shown for its existence, it would cease to be sin. Our only definition of sin is that given in the word of God; it is "the transgression of the law;" it is the outworking of a principle at war with the great law of love which is the foundation of the divine government.

Chapter 19
Sin Is Allegiance to Satan and Requires Death

Proverbs 14:34 Righteousness exalts a nation, but sin is a reproach to any people.

Ezekiel 18:20 The soul who sins shall die.

Ezekiel 33:11 Turn, turn from your evil ways! for why should you die?

Malachi 2:17 You have wearied the LORD with your words; yet you say, "In what way have we wearied Him?" In that you say, "Everyone who does evil is good in the sight of the LORD, and He delights in them," or, "Where is the God of justice?"

Matthew 7:26-27 Now everyone who hears these sayings of Mine, and does not do them, will be like a foolish man who built his house on the sand; and the rain descended, the floods came, and the winds blew and beat on that house; and it fell. And great was its fall.

Matthew 18: 8-9 If your hand or foot causes you to sin, cut it off and cast it from you. It is better for you to enter into life lame or maimed, rather than having two hands or two feet, to be cast into the everlasting fire. And if your eye causes you to sin, pluck it out and cast it from you. It is better for you to enter into life with one eye, rather than having two eyes, to be cast into hell fire.

John 3:20-21 For everyone practicing evil hates the light and does not come to the light, lest his deeds should be exposed. But he who does the truth comes to the light, that his deeds may be clearly seen, that they have been done in God.

John 8:34 Most assuredly, I say to you, whoever commits sin is a slave of sin.

Romans 6:2023 For when you were slaves of sin, you were free in regard to righteousness. What fruit did you have then in the things of which you are now ashamed? For the end of those things is death…. For the wages of sin is death, but the gift of God is eternal life in Christ Jesus our Lord.

Romans 7:11 For sin, taking occasion by the commandment, deceived me, and by it killed me.

Romans 8:3 For what the law could not do in that it was weak through the flesh, God did by sending His own Son in the likeness of sinful flesh, on account of sin: He condemned sin in the flesh.

Romans 8:6–8 For to be carnally minded is death, but to be spiritually minded is life and peace. Because the carnal mind is enmity against God; for it is not subject to the law of God, nor indeed can it be. So then, those who are in the flesh cannot please God.

Romans 8:13 For if you live according to the flesh you will die; but if by the Spirit you put to death the deeds of the body, you will live.

Ephesians 5:3-7 But fornication and all uncleanness or covetousness, let it not even be named among you, as is fitting for saints; neither filthiness, nor foolish talking, nor coarse jesting, which are not fitting, but rather giving of thanks. For this you know, that no fornicator, unclean person, nor covetous man, who is an idolater, has any inheritance in the kingdom of Christ and God. Let no one deceive you with empty words, for because of these things the wrath of God comes upon the sons of disobedience. Therefore do not be partakers with them.

Hebrews 3:18 And to whom did He swear that they would not enter His rest, but to those who did not obey?

Hebrews 4:6 Those to whom it was first preached did not enter because of disobedience.

1 John 1:6 If we say that we have fellowship with Him, and walk in darkness, we lie and do not practice the truth.

1 John 3:8 He who sins is of the devil, for the devil has sinned from the beginning. For this purpose the Son of God was manifested, that He might destroy the works of the devil.

1 John 3:10 In this the children of the devil are manifest: Whoever does not practice righteousness is not of God, nor is he who does not love his brother.

Romans 12:21 Do not be overcome by evil, but overcome evil with good.

Hebrews 3:12 Beware, brethren, lest there be in any of you an evil heart of unbelief in departing from the living God; but exhort one another daily, while it is called "Today," lest any of you be hardened through the deceitfulness of sin.

James 1:14 Each one is tempted when he is drawn away by his own desires and enticed. Then, when desire has conceived, it gives birth to sin, and sin, when it is full-grown, brings forth death.

SC 13 He who had been one with God, felt in His soul the awful separation that sin makes between God and man. This wrung from His lips the anguished cry, "My God, My God, why has Thou forsaken Me?" (Matt 27:46) It was the burden of sin, the sense of its terrible enormity, of its separation of the soul from God – it was this that broke the heart of the Son of God.

SC 17 After his sin, he [Adam] could no longer find joy in holiness, and he sought to hide from the presence of God. Such is still the condition of the unrenewed heart. It is not in harmony with God, and finds no joy in communion with Him. The sinner could not be happy in God's presence; he would shrink from the companionship of holy beings. Could he be permitted to enter heaven, it would have no joy for him…. His thoughts, his interests, his motives, would be alien to those that actuate the sinless dwellers there.

SC 31 But let none deceive themselves with the thought that God, in His great love and mercy, will yet save even the rejectors of His grace. The exceeding sinfulness of sin can be estimated only in the light of the cross. When men urge that God is too good to cast off the sinner, let them look to Calvary. It was because there was no other way in which man could be saved, because without this sacrifice it was impossible for the human race to escape from the defiling power of sin, and be restored to communion with holy beings – impossible for them again to become partakers of spiritual life – it was because of this that Christ took upon Himself the guilt of the disobedient and suffered in the sinner's stead.

SC 71 When the mind dwells upon self, it is turned away from Christ, the source of strength and life. Hence it is Satan's constant effort to keep the attention diverted from the Saviour and thus prevent the union and communion of the soul with Christ.

SC 72 He [Christ] bound humanity to Himself by a tie of love that can never be broken by any power save the choice of man himself. Satan will constantly present allurements to induce us to break this tie – to choose to separate ourselves from Christ.

DA 125 The tempter can never compel us to do evil. He cannot control minds unless they are yielded to his control. The will must consent, faith must let go its hold on Christ, before Satan can exercise his power upon us. But every sinful desire we cherish affords him a foothold. Every point in which we fail of meeting the divine standard is an open door by which he can enter to tempt and destroy us. And every failure or defeat on our part gives occasion for him to reproach Christ.

GC 22-23 Jesus, looking down to the last generation, saw the world involved in a deception similar to that which caused the destruction of Jerusalem. The great sin of the Jews was their rejection of Christ; the great sin of the Christian world would be their rejection of the law of God, the foundation of His government in heaven and earth. The precepts of Jehovah would be despised and set at naught. Millions in bondage to sin, slaves of Satan, doomed to suffer the second death, would refuse to listen to the words of truth in their day of visitation. Terrible blindness! Strange infatuation!

PP 55 Satan represented to the holy pair that they would be gainers by breaking the law of God. Do we not today hear similar reasoning? Many talk of the narrowness of those who obey God's commandments, while they themselves claim to have broader ideas and to enjoy greater liberty.

RH December 24, 1889 Every day that you remain in sin, you are in Satan's ranks; and should you sicken and die without repentance, you would be lost.

1T 186-187 The heart must be purified from sins which have so long shut out Jesus…. God leads His people on, step by step. He brings them up to different points calculated to manifest what is in their heart…. Here they have opportunity to see what is in their hearts that shuts out Jesus. They prize something higher than the truth, and their hearts are not prepared to receive Jesus.

MB 62 If you cling to self, refusing to yield your will to God, you are choosing death. To sin, wherever found, God is a consuming fire. If you choose sin, and refuse to separate from it, the presence of God, which consumes sin, must consume you.

Chapter 20
True Repentance Forsakes Sin

Proverbs 28:13   He who covers his sins will not prosper, but whoever confesses and forsakes them will have mercy.

Ezekiel 18:30-31   "Therefore I will judge you, O house of Israel, every one according to his ways," says the Lord God. "Repent, and turn from all your transgressions, so that iniquity will not be your ruin. Cast away from you all the transgressions which you have committed, and get yourselves a new heart and a new spirit. For why should you die, O house of Israel?"

Matthew 9:13   I do not come to call the righteous, but sinners, to repentance.

Romans 8:1   There is therefore now no condemnation to them which are in Christ Jesus, who do not walk according to the flesh, but according to the Spirit.

1 John 1:9   If we confess our sins, He is faithful and just to forgive us our sins, and to cleanse us from all unrighteousness.

2 Corinthians 7:10   For godly sorrow produces repentance leading to salvation, not to be regretted; but the sorrow of the world produces death.

SC 23   Repentance includes sorrow for sin and a turning away from it. We shall not renounce sin unless we see its sinfulness; until we turn away from it in heart, there will be no real change in the life.

SC 23   There are many who fail to understand the true nature of repentance. Multitudes sorrow that they have sinned and even make an outward reformation because they fear that their wrongdoing will bring suffering upon themselves. But this is not repentance in the Bible sense. They lament the suffering rather than the sin. Such was the grief of Esau when he saw that the birthright was lost to him forever. Balaam, terrified by the angel standing in his pathway with drawn sword, acknowledged his guilt lest he should lose his life; but there was no genuine repentance for sin, no conversion of purpose, no abhorrence of evil.

SC 24 But when the heart yields to the influence of the Spirit of God, the conscience will be quickened, and the sinner will discern something of the depth and sacredness of God's Holy law, the foundation of His government in heaven and earth.... The sinner has a sense of the righteousness of Jehovah and feels the terror of appearing, in his own guilt and uncleanness, before the Searcher of hearts. He sees the love of God, the beauty of holiness, the joy of purity; he longs to be cleansed and to be restored to communion with Heaven.

SC 24-25 The prayer of David after his fall, illustrates the nature of true sorrow for sin. His repentance was sincere and deep. There was no effort to palliate his guilt; no desire to escape the judgment threatened. David saw the enormity of his transgression; he saw the defilement of his soul; he loathed his sin. It was not for pardon only that he prayed, but for purity of heart. He longed for the joy of holiness – to be restored to harmony and communion with God.

SC 38 The only reason why we do not have remission of sins that are past is that we are not willing to humble our hearts and comply with the conditions of the word of truth.

SC 39 Confession will not be acceptable to God without sincere repentance and reformation. There must be decided changes in the life; everything offensive to God must be put away. This will be the result of genuine sorrow for sin.

DA 300 We often sorrow because our evil deeds bring unpleasant consequences to ourselves; but this is not repentance. Real sorrow for sin is the result of the working of the Holy Spirit. The Spirit reveals the ingratitude of the heart that has slighted and grieved the Savior, and brings us in contrition to the foot of the cross. By every sin Jesus is wounded afresh; and as we look upon Him whom we have pierced, we mourn for the sins that have brought anguish

114

upon Him. Such mourning will lead to the renunciation of sin.

DA 555-556 No repentance is genuine that does not work reformation. The righteousness of Christ is not a cloak to cover unconfessed and unforsaken sin; it is a principle of life that transforms the character and controls the conduct. Holiness is wholeness of God; it is the entire surrender of heart and life to the indwelling principles of heaven.

GC 483 All who have truly repented of sin, and by faith claimed the blood of Christ as their atoning sacrifice, have had pardon entered against their names in the books of heaven; as they have become partakers of the righteousness of Christ, and their characters are found to be in harmony with the law of God, their sins will be blotted out, and they themselves will be accounted worthy of eternal life.

1SM 350 There are hindrances to be removed. Wrong feelings have been cherished, and there have been pride, self-sufficiency, impatience, and murmurings. All these separate us from God. Sins must be confessed; there must be a deeper work of grace in the heart.

1SM 393 In order to obtain the righteousness of Christ, it is necessary for the sinner to know what that repentance is which works a radical change of mind and spirit and action. The work of transformation must begin in the heart, and manifest its power through every faculty of the being; but man is not capable of originating such a repentance as this, and can experience it alone through Christ.

3SM 190-191 To be pardoned in the way that Christ pardons, is not only to be forgiven, but to be renewed in the spirit of our mind. The Lord says, "A new heart will I give unto thee." The image of Christ is to be stamped upon the very mind, heart, and soul. The apostle says, "But we have the mind of Christ." (1 Cor. 2:16). Without the transforming process which can come alone through divine power, the original propensities to sin are left in the heart in all their strength, to forge new chains, to impose a slavery that can never be broken by human power. But men can never enter heaven with their old tastes, inclinations, idols, ideas, and theories. Heaven would be no place of joy to them; for everything would be in collision with their tastes, appetites, and inclinations, and painfully opposed to their natural and cultivated traits of character.

Chapter 21
Grace of God Is No Excuse to Sin

Romans 1:18-20   For the wrath of God is revealed from heaven against all ungodliness and unrighteousness of men, who suppress the truth in unrighteousness, because what may be known of God is manifest in them, for God has shown it to them. For since the creation of the world His invisible attributes are clearly seen, being understood by the things that are made, even His eternal power and Godhead, so that they are without excuse, because, although they knew God, they did not glorify Him as God, nor were thankful, but became futile in their thoughts, and their foolish hearts were darkened. Professing to be wise, they became fools, and changed the glory of the incorruptible God into an image made like corruptible man – and birds and four-footed animals and creeping things.

Romans 6:1   Shall we continue in sin that grace may abound? Certainly not! How shall we who died to sin live any longer in it?

Titus 2:11-14   For the grace of God that brings salvation has appeared to all men, teaching us that, denying ungodliness and worldly lusts, we should live soberly, righteously, and godly in the present age, looking for the blessed hope and glorious appearing of our great God and Savior Jesus Christ, who gave Himself for us, that He might redeem us from every lawless deed and purify for Himself His own special people, zealous for good works.

1 John 3:6   Whoever abides in Him does not sin.

James 1:22   But be doers of the word, and not hearers only, deceiving yourselves.

Jude 1:4   For certain men have crept in unnoticed, who long ago were marked out for this condemnation, ungodly men, who turn the grace of our God into licentiousness and deny the only Lord God and our Lord Jesus Christ.

117

RH Sept 15, 1896 But God does not use His grace to make His law of none effect, or to take the place of His law.... God's grace and the law of His kingdom are in perfect harmony; they walk hand in hand. His grace makes it possible for us to draw nigh to Him by faith. By receiving it, and letting it work in our lives, we testify to the validity of the law; we exalt the law and make it honorable by carrying out its living principles through the power of the grace of Christ; and by rendering pure, whole-hearted obedience to God's law, we witness before the universe of heaven, and before an apostate world that is making void the law of God, to the power of redemption.

1SM 361 The Holiness people have gone to great extremes on this point. With great zeal they have taught "Only believe in Christ, and be saved; but away with the law of God." This is not the teaching of the Word of God.... Christ must be lifted up, because He is a Saviour who forgiveth transgression, iniquity, and sin, but will by no means clear the guilty and unrepentant soul.

1SM 382 When it is in the heart to obey God, when efforts are put forth to this end, Jesus accepts this disposition and effort as man's best service, and He makes up for the deficiency with His own divine merit. But He will not accept those who claim to have faith in Him, and yet are disloyal to His Father's commandments. We hear a great deal about faith, but we need to hear a great deal more about works. Many are deceiving their own souls by living an easy-going, accommodating, crossless religion. But Jesus says, "If any man will come after me, let him deny himself, and take up his cross, and follow me."

COL 316 The love of God does not lead Him to excuse sin. He did not excuse it in Satan; He did not excuse it in Adam or in Cain; nor will He excuse it in any other of the children of men. He will not connive at our sins or overlook our defects of character. He expects us to overcome in His name.

Chapter 22
Christ's Robe of Righteousness Doesn't Cover Sin

[Christ's robe of righteousness is exactly what it says. It is His righteousness given to us - we will live a righteous life. God is not a liar – He cannot call us righteous while we sin. When we sin, we must first throw off His robe, depart from Him, and choose our sinful desire – which is Satan.]

Exodus 34:7   Keeping mercy for thousands, forgiving iniquity and transgression and sin, by no means clearing the guilty.

Matthew 10:26   For there is nothing covered that will not be revealed, and hidden that will not be known.

Isaiah 61:10   I will greatly rejoice in the LORD, my soul shall be joyful in my God; for He has clothed me with the garments of salvation, He has covered me with the robe of righteousness, as a bridegroom decks himself with ornaments, and as a bride adorns herself with her jewels.

Jeremiah 4:14   O Jerusalem, wash your heart from wickedness, that you may be saved. How long shall your evil thoughts lodge within you?

Ezekiel 36:25-27   Then I will sprinkle clean water on you, and you shall be clean; I will cleanse you from all your filthiness and from all your idols. I will give you a new heart and put a new spirit within you; I will take the heart of stone out of your flesh and give you a heart of flesh. I will put My Spirit within you and cause you to walk in My statutes, and you will keep My judgments and do them.

Ephesians 5:26-27   That He might sanctify and cleanse her with the washing of water by the word, that He might present her to Himself a glorious church, not having spot or wrinkle or any such thing, but that she should be holy and without blemish.

1 Corinthians 6:9-11   Do you not know that the unrighteous will not inherit the kingdom of God? Do not be deceived.... And such were some of you. But you were washed, you were sanctified, you were justified in the name of the Lord Jesus Christ and in the Spirit of our God.

Hebrews 10:22 Let us draw near with a true heart in full assurance of faith, having our hearts sprinkled from an evil conscience and our bodies washed with pure water.

2 Peter 3:14 Therefore, beloved, looking forward to these things, be diligent to be found by Him in peace, without spot and blameless.

Revelation 3:5 He who overcomes shall be clothed in white garments, and I will not blot out his name from the Book of Life; but I will confess his name before My Father and before His angels.

Revelation 3:18 I counsel you to buy from Me gold refined in the fire, that you may be rich; and white garments, that you may be clothed, that the shame of your nakedness may not be revealed; and anoint your eyes with eye salve, that you may see.

Revelation 7:14 These are the ones who come out of the great tribulation, and washed their robes and made them white in the blood of the Lamb.

Revelation 16:15 Behold, I am coming as a thief. Blessed is he who watches, and keeps his garments, lest he walk naked and they see his shame.

Revelation 19:8 And to her it was granted to be arrayed in fine linen, clean and bright, for the fine linen is the righteous acts of the saints.

DA 555-556 No repentance is genuine that does not work reformation. The righteousness of Christ is not a cloak to cover unconfessed and unforsaken sin; it is a principle of life that transforms the character and controls the conduct. Holiness is wholeness for God; it is the entire surrender of heart and life to the indwelling principles of heaven.

1T 160 He demands all. When we are brought to yield to His claims, and give up all, then, and not till then, will He throw around us His arms of mercy. But what do we give when we give all? A sin-polluted soul for Jesus to purify, to cleanse by His mercy, and to save from death by His matchless love.

5T 220-221   God has made ample provision that we may stand perfect in His grace, wanting in nothing, waiting for the appearing of our Lord. Are you ready? Have you the wedding garment on? That garment will never cover deceit, impurity, corruption, or hypocrisy. The eye of God is upon you. It is a discerner of the thoughts and intents of the heart. We may conceal our sins from the eyes of men, but we can hide nothing from our Maker.

COL 310-312   The white robe of innocence was worn by our first parents when they were placed by God in holy Eden. They lived in perfect conformity to the will of God. All the strength of their affections was given to their heavenly Father. A beautiful soft light, the light of God, enshrouded the holy pair. This robe of light was a symbol of their spiritual garments of heavenly innocence. Had they remained true to God it would ever have continued to enshroud them. But when sin entered, they severed their connection with God, and the light that had encircled them departed. Naked and ashamed, they tried to supply the place of the heavenly garments by sewing together fig leaves for a covering. This is what the transgressors of God's law have done ever since the day of Adam and Eve's disobedience. They have sewed together fig leaves to cover the nakedness caused by transgression. They have worn the garments of their own devising, by works of their own they have tried to cover their sins, and make themselves acceptable with God. But this they can never do. Nothing can man devise to supply the place of his lost robe of innocence…. When we submit ourselves to Christ, the heart is united with His heart, the will is merged in His will, the mind becomes one with His mind, the thoughts are brought into captivity to Him; we live His life. This is what it means to be clothed with the garment of His righteousness. Then as the Lord looks upon us He sees, not the fig-leaf garment, not the nakedness and deformity of sin, but His own robe of righteousness, which is perfect obedience to the law of Jehovah. The guests at the marriage feast were inspected by the king. Only those were accepted who had obeyed his requirements and put on the wedding garment. So it is with the guests at the gospel feast. All must pass the scrutiny of the great King, and only those are received who have put on the robe of Christ's righteousness. Righteousness is right doing, and it is by their deeds that all will be judged. Our characters are revealed by what we do. The works show whether the faith is genuine.

COL 319 There will be no future probation in which to prepare for eternity. It is in this life that we are to put on the robe of Christ's righteousness. This is our only opportunity to form characters for the home which Christ has made ready for those who obey His commandments.

AA 388 Paul pleaded with those who had once known in their lives the power of God, to return to their first love of gospel truth. With unanswerable arguments he set before them their privilege of becoming free men and women in Christ, through whose atoning grace all who make full surrender are clothed with the robe of His righteousness. He took the position that every soul who would be saved must have a genuine, personal experience in the things of God.

CCh 353 As the people of God afflict their souls before Him, pleading for purity of heart, the command is given, "Take away the filthy garments" from them, and the encouraging words are spoken, "Behold, I have caused thine iniquity to pass from thee, and I will clothe thee with change of raiment." The spotless robe of Christ's righteousness is placed upon the tried, tempted, yet faithful children of God.... They have resisted the wiles of the deceiver; they have not been turned from their loyalty by the dragon's roar. Now they are eternally secure.

RH September 19, 1899 Christ declares, "He that will come after Me, let him deny himself, and take up his cross, and follow Me." Those who have on the wedding garment, the robe of Christ's righteousness, will not question whether they should lift the cross, and follow in the footsteps of the Saviour. Willingly and cheerfully they will obey His commands. Souls are perishing out of Christ.

CT 340-341 Professed Christians who are superficial in character and religious experience are used by the tempter as his decoys. This class are always ready for the gatherings for pleasure or sport, and their influence attracts others.... They do not discern that these entertainments are really Satan's banquet, prepared to keep souls from accepting the call to the marriage supper of the Lamb and preventing them from receiving the white robe of character, which is the righteousness of Christ.

FW 106 It is the righteousness of Christ that makes the penitent sinner acceptable to God and works his justification. However sinful has been his life, if he believes in Jesus as his personal Saviour, he stands before God in the spotless robes of Christ's imputed righteousness. The sinner so recently dead in trespasses and sins is quickened by faith in Christ. He sees by faith that Jesus is his Saviour, and alive forevermore, able to save unto "the uttermost [all] that come unto God by Him." In the atonement made for him the believer sees such breadth and length and height and depth of efficiency – sees such completeness of salvation, purchased at such infinite cost, that his soul is filled with praise and thanksgiving. He sees as in a glass the glory of the Lord and is changed into the same image as by the Spirit of the Lord. He sees the robe of Christ's righteousness, woven in the loom of heaven, wrought by His obedience.... Perfection through our own good works we can never attain. The soul who sees Jesus by faith, repudiates his own righteousness. He sees himself as incomplete, his repentance insufficient, his strongest faith but feebleness, his most costly sacrifice as meager, and he sinks in humility at the foot of the cross. But a voice speaks to him from the oracles of God's word. In amazement he hears the message, "Ye are complete in Him." Now all is at rest in his soul. No longer must he strive to find some worthiness in himself, some meritorious deed by which to gain the favor of God.

1SM 366 But while God can be just, and yet justify the sinner through the merits of Christ, no man can cover his soul with the garments of Christ's righteousness while practicing known sins, or neglecting known duties. God requires the entire surrender of the heart, before justification can take place; and in order for man to retain justification, there must be continual obedience, through active, living faith that works by love and purifies the soul.

MS 142, 1899 Christ is able to save to the uttermost all who come to Him in faith. He will cleanse them from all defilement if they will let Him. But if they cling to their sins, they cannot possibly be saved; for Christ's righteousness covers no sin unrepented of.

OHC 214 Sanctification is a state of holiness, without and within, being holy and without reserve the Lord's, not in form, but in truth. Every impurity of thought, every lustful passion, separates the soul from God; for Christ can never put His robe of righteousness upon a sinner, to hide his deformity.

SD 13 Only by faithful repentance will their sins be forgiven; for God will never cover evil with the robe of His righteousness.

4T 185 Those who seek to cloak sin, and make it appear less aggravating to the mind of the offender, are doing the work of the false prophets, and may expect the retributive wrath of God to follow such a course.

4T 294 Here is a work for man to do. He must face the mirror, God's law, discern the defects of his moral character, and put away his sins, washing his robe of character in the blood of the Lamb.

Chapter 23
Danger of Progressively Sinning Less

Proverbs 5:22   His own iniquities entrap the wicked man, and he is caught in the cords of his sins.

Romans 8:7   Because the carnal mind is enmity against God; for it is not subject to the law of God, nor indeed can be.

1 Thessalonians 4:7   For God did not call us to uncleanness, but in holiness.

Hebrews 10:26-27   For if we sin willfully after we have received the knowledge of the truth, there no longer remains a sacrifice for sins, but a certain fearful expectation of judgment, and fiery indignation which will devour the adversaries.

Hebrews 12:1   Therefore we also, since we are surrounded by so great a cloud of witnesses, let us lay aside every weight, and the sin which so easily ensnares us, and let us run with endurance the race that is set before us.

James 2:10   For whoever shall keep the whole law, and yet stumble in one point, he is guilty of all.

1 John 2:3-6   Now by this we know that we know Him, if we keep His commandments. He who says, "I know Him," and does not keep His commandments, is a liar, and the truth is not in him. But whoever keeps His word, truly the love of God is perfected in him. By this we know that we are in Him. He who says he abides in Him ought himself also to walk just as He walked.

1 John 2:15-16   Do not love the world or the things in the world. If anyone loves the world, the love of the Father is not in him. For all that is in the world – the lust of the flesh, the lust of the eyes, and the pride of life – is not of the Father but is of the world.

1 John 3:8-9   He who sins is of the devil, for the devil has sinned from the beginning. For this purpose the Son of God was manifested, that He might destroy the works of the devil. Whoever has been born of God does not sin, for His seed remains in him; and he cannot sin, because he has been born of God.

2SM 51   We must beware of the pretended holiness that permits transgression of the law of God.

RH June 8, 1886   God will not be trifled with... God is a sin-hating God; and those who will encourage the sinner, saying, It is well with thee, God will curse.

RH March 10, 1904   He who has not sufficient faith in Christ to believe that He can keep him from sinning, has not the faith that will give him an entrance into the kingdom of God.

5T 540   That religion which makes of sin a light matter, dwelling upon the love of God to the sinner regardless of his actions, only encourages the sinner to believe that God will receive him while he continues in that which he knows to be sin.   This is what some are doing who profess to believe present truth.   The truth is kept apart from the life, and that is the reason it has no power to convict and convert the soul.

SC 32-34   Do not put off the work of forsaking sins and seeking purity of heart through Jesus.   Here is where thousands upon thousands have erred to their eternal loss.... There is a terrible danger – a danger not sufficiently understood – in delaying to yield to the pleading voice of God's Holy Spirit, in choosing to live in sin; for such this delay really is.   Sin, however small it may be esteemed, can be indulged in only at the peril of infinite loss.   What we do not overcome, will overcome us and work out our destruction.   Adam and Eve persuaded themselves that in so small a matter as eating of the forbidden fruit there could not result such terrible consequences as God had declared.   But this small matter was the transgression of God's immutable and holy law, and it separated man from God and opened the floodgates of death and untold woe upon our world.... Calvary stands as a memorial of the amazing sacrifice required to atone for the transgression of the divine law.   Let us not regard sin as a trivial thing. Every act of transgression, every neglect or rejection of the grace of Christ, is reacting upon yourself; it is hardening the heart, depraving the will, benumbing the understanding, and not only making you less inclined to yield, but less capable of yielding, to the tender pleading of God's Holy Spirit. Many are quieting a troubled conscience with the thought that they can change a course of evil when they choose; that they can trifle with the invitations of mercy, and yet be again and again impressed. They think that after doing despite to the Spirit of grace, after casting their influence on the side of Satan, in a moment of terrible extremity they can change their course. But this is not easily done. The experience, the education, of a lifetime, has so thoroughly molded the character that few then desire to receive the image of Jesus. Even one wrong trait of character, one sinful desire, persistently cherished, will eventually neutralize all the power of the gospel. Every sinful indulgence strengthens the soul's aversion to God. The man who manifests an infidel hardihood, or a stolid indifference to divine truth, is but reaping the harvest of that which he has himself sown. In all the Bible there is not a more fearful warning against trifling with evil than the words of the wise man that the sinner "shall be holden with the cords of his sins." Proverbs 5:22

MB 94 The strongest bulwark of vice in our world is not the iniquitous life of the abandoned sinner or the degraded outcast; it is that life which otherwise appears virtuous, honorable, and noble, but in which one sin is fostered, one vice indulged.

1SM 213 There is no safety or repose nor justification in transgression of the law. Man cannot hope to stand innocent before God, and at peace with Him through the merits of Christ, while he continues in sin. He must cease to transgress, and become loyal and true.

1SM 327-328 We are to surrender our hearts to God, that He may renew and sanctify us, and fit us for His heavenly court. We are not to wait for some special time, but today we are to give ourselves to Him, refusing to be the servants of sin. Do you imagine you can leave off sin a little at a time? Oh, leave the accursed thing at once! Hate the things that Christ hates, love the things that Christ loves. Has He not by His death and suffering made provision for your cleansing from sin? When we begin to realize that we are sinners, and fall on the Rock to be broken, the everlasting arms are placed about us, and we are brought close to the heart of Jesus. Then we shall be charmed with His loveliness, and disgusted with our own righteousness.

1SM 394-395 The Lord would have His people sound in the faith – not ignorant of the great salvation so abundantly provided for them. They are not to look forward, thinking that at some future time a great work is to be done for them; for the work is now complete…. He makes an end of the controlling power of sin in the heart, and the life and character of the believer testify to the genuine character of the grace of Christ. To those that ask Him, Jesus imparts the Holy Spirit; for it is necessary that every believer should be delivered from pollution, as well as from the curse and condemnation of the law. Through the work of the Holy Spirit, the sanctification of the truth, the believer becomes fitted for the courts of heaven; for Christ works within us, and His righteousness is upon us.

RH March 2, 1897 Many have in a great measure failed to receive the former rain. They have not obtained all the benefits that God has thus provided for them. They expect that the lack will be supplied by the latter rain. When the richest abundance of grace shall be bestowed, they intend to open their hearts to receive it. They are making a terrible mistake. The work that God has begun in the human heart in giving his light and knowledge, must be continually going forward. Every individual must realize his own necessity. The heart must be emptied of every defilement, and cleansed for the indwelling of the Spirit. It was by the confession and forsaking of sin, by earnest prayer and consecration of themselves to God, that the early disciples prepared for the outpouring of the Holy Spirit on the day of Pentecost. The same work, only in greater degree, must be done now. Then the human agent had only to ask for the blessing, and wait for the Lord to perfect the work concerning him. It is God who began the work, and he will finish his work, making man complete in Jesus Christ. But there must be no neglect of the grace represented by the former rain. Only those who are living up to the light they have, will receive greater light. Unless we are daily advancing in the exemplification of the active Christian virtues, we shall not recognize the manifestations of the Holy Spirit in the latter rain. It may be falling on hearts all around us, but we shall not discern or receive it.

4T 534-535 Many who profess the faith know not what true conversion is. They have no experience in communion with the Father through Jesus Christ, and have never felt the power of divine grace to sanctify the heart. Praying and sinning, sinning and praying, their lives are full of malice, deceit, envy, jealousy, and self-love. The prayers of this class are an abomination to God. True prayer engages the energies of the soul and affects the life.

5T 142 He who holds the truth in unrighteousness, who declares his belief in it, and yet wounds it every day by his inconsistent life, is surrendering himself to the service of Satan and leading souls to ruin.

ED 291 "Fools make a mock at sin." Proverbs 14:9. We should beware of treating sin as a light thing. Terrible is its power over the wrongdoer. "His own iniquities shall take the wicked himself, and he shall be holden with the cords of his sins." Proverbs 5:22. The greatest wrong done to a child or youth is to allow him to become fastened in the bondage of evil habit.

MB 138-139 In order to go in the path that leads to destruction, there is no need of searching for the way; for the gate is wide, and the way is broad, and the feet naturally turn into the path that ends in death. But the way to life is narrow and the entrance is strait. If you cling to any besetting sin you will find the way too narrow for you to enter. Your own ways, your own will, your evil habits and practices, must be given up if you would keep the way of the Lord.

DA 313 If one sin is cherished in the soul, or one wrong practice retained in the life, the whole being is contaminated. The man becomes an instrument of unrighteousness.

GC 489 If those who hide and excuse their faults could see how Satan exults over them, how he taunts Christ and holy angles with their course, they would make haste to confess their sins and to put them away.

TMK 248 If you suppose for a moment that God will treat sin lightly or make provisions or exemptions so that you can go on in committing sin, and the soul suffer no penalty for thus doing, it is a terrible delusion of Satan.

Chapter 24
Danger of Unknown Sin

[What happens if there is unknown sin in heaven? Satan's unknown sin brought ruin to heaven the first time, and Eve's unknown sin brought ruin to earth. Sin must be completely eradicated in our character here on earth or there will be unknown sin in heaven again, and heaven will be ruined again. We can only be safe by distrusting self, abiding in Jesus, and trustingly obeying forever.]

Leviticus 5:17-19   If a person sins, and commits any of these things which are forbidden to be done by the commandments of the LORD, though he does not know it, yet he is guilty and shall bear his iniquity. And he shall bring to the priest a ram without blemish from the flock, with your valuation, as a trespass offering. So the priest shall make atonement for him regarding his ignorance in which he erred and did not know it, and it shall be forgiven him. It is a trespass offering; he has certainly trespassed against the LORD.

Psalms 139: 23-24   Search me, O God, and know my heart; try me, and know my anxieties; and see if there is any wicked way in me, and lead me in the way everlasting.

Proverbs 30:12   There is a generation that is pure in its own eyes, yet is not washed from its filthiness.

Luke 12:47-48   And that servant who knew his master's will, and did not prepare himself or do according to his will, shall be beaten with many stripes. But he who did not know, yet committed things deserving of stripes, shall be beaten with few.

John 7:17   If anyone wills to do His will, he shall know concerning the doctrine.

John 8:12   The way of the wicked is like darkness; they do not know what makes them stumble.

John 12:46   I have come as a light into the world, that whoever believes in Me should not abide in darkness.

1 Corinthians 1:30   But of Him you are in Christ Jesus, who became for us wisdom from God – and righteousness and sanctification and redemption.

2 Corinthians 11:3   But I fear, lest somehow, as the serpent deceived Eve by his craftiness, so your minds may be corrupted from the simplicity that is in Christ.

Ephesians 2:10   For we are His workmanship, created in Christ Jesus for good works, which God prepared beforehand that we should walk in them.

Ephesians 5:17   Therefore do not be unwise, but understand what the will of the Lord is.

Colossians 2:9-10   For in Him dwells all the fullness of the Godhead bodily; and you are complete in Him, who is the head of all principality and power.

2 Timothy 3:16-17   All Scripture is given by inspiration of God, and is profitable   for   doctrine,   for   reproof,   for correction, for instruction in righteousness, that the man of God may be complete, thoroughly equipped for every good work.

2 Thessalonians 3:3   But the Lord is faithful, who will establish you and guard you from the evil one.

James 2:10   For whoever shall keep the whole law, and yet stumble in one point, he is guilty of all.

2 Peter 1:3-4   As His divine power has given to us all things that pertain to life and godliness, through the knowledge of Him who called us by glory and virtue, by which have been given to us exceedingly great and of precious promises, that through these you may be partakes of the divine nature, having escaped the corruption that is in the world through lust.

RH December 24, 1889   Every day that you remain in sin, you are in Satan's ranks; and should you sicken and die without repentance, you would be lost.

RH April 24, 1900   We must learn of Christ. We must know what He is to those He has ransomed. We must realize that through belief in Him it is our privilege to be partakers of the divine nature, and so escape the corruption that is in the world through lust. Then we are cleansed from all sin, all defects of character. We need not retain one sinful propensity. Christ is the sin-bearer; John pointed the people to Him, saying, "Behold, the Lamb of God, which taketh away the sin of the world."

ST March 17, 1890 One sin unrepented of is enough to close the gates of heaven against you. It was because man could not be saved with one stain of sin upon him, that Jesus came to die on Calvary's cross.

RH November 24, 1896 He will quicken your conscience, renew your heart, sanctify your affections, purify your thoughts, and set all your powers at work for Him. Every motive and every thought will be brought into captivity to Jesus Christ.

GC 496 Lucifer himself did not at first see whither he was drifting; he did not understand the real nature of his feelings.

GC 597 Ignorance is no excuse for error or sin, when there is every opportunity to know the will of God. A man is traveling and comes to a place where there are several roads and a guideboard indicating where each one leads. If he disregards the guideboard, and takes whichever road seems to him to be right, he may be ever so sincere, but will in all probability find himself on the wrong road.

1SM 218 Not one of these precepts can be broken without disloyalty to the God of Heaven. The least deviation from its requirements, by neglect or willful transgression, is sin, and every sin exposes the sinner to the wrath of God.

2T 447 God is too pure to behold iniquity. A sin is just as grievous in His sight in one case as in another. No exception will be made by an impartial God.

2SM 379 The least transgression of God's law brings guilt upon the transgressor, and without earnest repentance and forsaking of sin he will surely become an apostate.

2SM 352-353 For thousands of years Satan has been experimenting upon the properties of the human mind, and he has learned to know it well. By his subtle workings in these last days, he is linking the human mind with his own, imbuing it with his thoughts; and he is doing this work in so deceptive a manner that those who accept his guidance know not that they are being led by him at his will. The great deceiver hopes so to confuse the minds of men and women, that none but his voice will be heard.

SC 40 When sin has deadened the moral perceptions, the wrongdoer does not discern the defects of his character nor realize the enormity of the evil he has committed; and unless he yields to the convicting power of the Holy Spirit he remains in partial blindness to his sin. His confessions are not sincere and in earnest. To every acknowledgment of his guilt he adds an apology in excuse of his course, declaring that if it had not been for certain circumstances he would not have done this or that for which he is reproved.

RH November 15, 1898 The Lord does not save sinners by abrogating his law, the foundation of his government in heaven and earth. God is a judge, the guardian of justice. The transgression of his law in a single instance, in the smallest particular, is sin. God cannot dispense with his law, he cannot do away with its smallest item, in order to pardon sin. The justice, the moral excellence, of the law must be maintained and vindicated before the heavenly universe. And that holy law could not be maintained at any smaller price than the death of the Son of God.

SD 76 As the life of the vine circulates through stem and cluster, descends into the lower fibers, and reaches to the topmost leaf, so will the grace and love of Christ burn and abound in the soul, sending its virtues to every part of the being, and pervading every exercise of body and mind.

1SM 380 Man is to cooperate with God, employing every power according to his God-given ability. He is not to be ignorant as to what are right practices in eating and drinking, and in all the habits of life.... We cannot afford to neglect one ray of life God has given. To be sluggish in our practice of those things which require diligence is to commit sin.

AA 284   The life-giving power of the Holy Spirit, proceeding from the Saviour, pervades the soul, renews the motives and affections, and brings even the thoughts into obedience to the will of God, enabling the receiver to bear the precious fruit of holy deeds.

PP 55 Eve really believed the words of Satan, but her belief did not save her from the penalty of sin. She disbelieved the words of God, and this was what led to her fall. In the judgment men will not be condemned because they conscientiously believed a lie, but because thy did not believe the truth, because they neglected the opportunity of learning what is truth.

PP 522 Satan deceives many with the plausible theory that God's love for His people is so great that He will excuse sin in them.

5T 294   The enemy is preparing for his last campaign against the church. He has so concealed himself from view that many can hardly believe that he exists, much less can they be convinced of his amazing activity and power. They have to a great extent forgotten his past record; and when he makes another advance move, they will not recognize him as their enemy, that old serpent, but they will consider him a friend, one who is doing a good work. Boasting of their independence they will, under his specious, bewitching influence, obey the worst impulses of the human heart and yet believe that God is leading them. Could their eyes be opened to distinguish their captain, they would see that they are not serving God, but the enemy of all righteousness. They would see that their boasted independence is one of the heaviest fetters Satan can rivet on unbalanced minds.

Chapter 25
Love for Mankind Warns of Sin

Isaiah 58:1 Cry aloud, spare not; lift up your voice like a trumpet; tell My people their transgression, and the house of Jacob their sins.

Ezekiel 3:18-21 When I say to the wicked, "You shall surely die," and you give him no warning, nor speak to warn the wicked from his wicked way, to save his life, that same wicked man shall die in his iniquity; but his blood I will require at your hand. Yet, if you warn the wicked, and he does not turn from his wickedness, nor from his wicked way, he shall die in his iniquity; but you have delivered your soul. Again, when a righteous man turns from his righteousness and commits iniquity, and I lay a stumbling block before him, he shall die; because you did not give him warning, he shall die in his sin, and his righteousness which he has done shall not be remembered; but his blood I will require at your hand. Nevertheless if you warn the righteous man that the righteous should not sin, and he does not sin, he shall surely live because he took warning; also you will have delivered your soul.

Matthew 28:19-20 Go therefore and make disciples of all the nations, baptizing them in the name of the Father and of the Son and of the Holy Spirit, teaching them to observe all things that I have commanded you; and lo, I am with you always, even to the end of the age.

Luke 21:14-15 Therefore settle it in your hearts not to meditate beforehand on what you will answer; for I will give you a mouth and wisdom which all your adversaries will not be able to contradict or resist.

Acts 1:8 But you shall receive power when the Holy Spirit has come upon you; and you shall be witnesses to Me in Jerusalem, and in all Judea and Samaria, and to the end of the earth.

Acts 4:31   They were all filled with the Holy Spirit, and they spoke the word of God with boldness.

Acts 20:27-31   For I have not shunned to declare to you the whole counsel of God.   Therefore take heed to yourselves and to all the flock, among which the Holy Spirit has made you overseers, to shepherd the church of God which He purchased with His own blood. For I know this, that after my departure savage wolves will come in among you, not sparing the flock.   Also from among yourselves men will rise up, speaking perverse things, to draw away the disciples after themselves. Therefore watch, and remember that for three years I did not cease to warn everyone night and day with tears.

Acts 26:17-18   I will deliver you from the Jewish people, as well as from the Gentiles, to whom I now send you, to open their eyes, in order to turn them from darkness to light, and from the power of Satan to God, that they may receive forgiveness of sins and an inheritance among those who are sanctified by faith in Me.

Galatians 6:1   Brethren, if a man is overtaken in any trespass, you who are spiritual restore such a one in a spirit of gentleness, considering yourself lest you also be tempted.

Colossians 1:27-29   To them God willed to make known what are the riches of the glory of this mystery among the Gentiles: which is Christ in you, the hope of glory.   Him we preach, warning every man and teaching every man in all wisdom, that we may present every man perfect in Christ Jesus. To this end I also labor, striving according to His working which works in me mightily.

2 Thessalonians 3:15   Yet do not count him as an enemy, but admonish him as a brother.

2 Timothy 1:7-8   For God has not given us a spirit of fear, but of power and of love and of a sound mind. Therefore do not be ashamed of the testimony of our Lord, nor of me His prisoner, but share with me in the sufferings for the gospel according to the power of God.

2 Timothy 4:2   Preach the word! Be ready in season and out of season.   Convince, rebuke, exhort, with all longsuffering and teaching.

Revelation 3:19   As many as I love, I rebuke and chasten. Therefore be zealous and repent.

SC 78-79   If we are clothed with the righteousness of Christ and are filled with the joy of His indwelling Spirit, we shall not be able to hold our peace. If we have tasted and seen that the Lord is good we shall have something to tell.... There will be an earnest longing that those around us may "behold the Lamb of God, which taketh away the sin of the world." John 1:29

SC 81   The love of Christ, revealed to us, makes us debtors to all who know Him not. God has given us light, not for ourselves alone, but to shed upon them.

DA 104   God does not send messengers to flatter the sinner. He delivers no message of peace to lull the unsanctified into fatal security. He lays heavy burdens upon the conscience of the wrongdoer, and pierces the soul with arrows of conviction. The ministering angels present to him the fearful judgments of God to deepen the sense of need, and prompt the cry, "What must I do to be saved?"

DA 806   Warn every soul that is in danger. Leave none to deceive themselves. Call sin by its right name. Declare what God has said in regard to lying, Sabbath-breaking, stealing, idolatry, and every other evil....In labor for the erring, let every eye be directed to Christ. Let the shepherds have a tender care for the flock of the Lord's pasture. Let them speak to the erring of the forgiving mercy of the Saviour. Let them encourage the sinner to repent, and believe in Him who can pardon.

AA 554-555   We are authorized to hold in the same estimation as did the beloved disciple those who claim to abide in Christ while living in transgression of God's law. There exist in these last days evils similar to those that threatened the prosperity of the early church; and the teachings of the apostle John on these points should be carefully heeded. "You must have charity" is the cry heard everywhere, especially from those who profess sanctification. But true charity is too pure to cover an unconfessed sin. While we are to love the souls for whom Christ died, we are to make no compromise with evil. We are not to unite with the rebellious and call this charity. God requires His people in this age of the world to stand for the right as unflinchingly as did John in opposition to soul-destroying errors.... His testimony in regard to the Saviour's life and death was clear and forcible. Out of the abundance of a heart overflowing with love for the Saviour he spoke; and no power could stay his words.

1SM 374 If you are willing to drift along with the current of evil, and do not cooperate with the heavenly agencies in restraining transgression in your family, and in the church, in order that everlasting righteousness may be brought in, you do not have faith. Faith works by love and purifies the soul.

DA 152 We should never give sanction to sin by our words or our deeds, our silence or our presence.

2SM 369-370 Let not those who have the truth as it is in Jesus give sanction, even by their silence, to the work of the mystery of iniquity. Let them never cease to sound the note of alarm.... The truth must not be hid, it must not be denied or disguised, but fully avowed, and boldly proclaimed.

2SM 371 You must not bring a railing accusation against any, whether individuals or churches. Learn to deal with minds as Christ did. Sharp things must sometimes be spoken; but be sure that the Holy Spirit of God is abiding in your heart before you speak the clear-cut truth; then let it cut its way. You are not to do the cutting.

2SM 402-404 Recently in the night season, my mind was impressed by the Holy Spirit with the thought that if the Lord is coming as soon as we believe He is, we ought to be even more active than we have been in years past in getting the truth before the people. In this connection my mind reverted to the activity of the Advent believers in 1843 and 1844. At that time there was much house-to-house visitation, and untiring efforts were made to warn the people of the things that are spoken of in God's Word. We should be putting forth even greater effort than was put forth by those who proclaimed the first angel's message so faithfully. We are rapidly approaching the end of this earth's history; and as we realize that Jesus is indeed coming soon, we shall be aroused to labor as never before. We are bidden to sound the alarm to the people. And in our own lives we are to show forth the power of truth and righteousness. The world is soon to meet the great Lawgiver over His broken law. Those only who turn from transgression to obedience can hope for pardon and peace. We are to raise the banner on which is inscribed, "The commandments of God, and the faith of Jesus." Obedience to God's law is the great issue. Let it not be put out of sight. We must strive to arouse church members, and those who make no profession, to see and obey the claims of the law of Heaven. We are to magnify this law and make it honorable…. Who among God's professing people will take up this sacred work, and labor for the souls who are perishing for lack of knowledge? The world must be warned.

1T 321   The forerunner of Christ's first advent was a very plain-spoken man. He rebuked sin, and called things by their right names. He laid the ax at the root of the tree…. In this fearful time, just before Christ is to come the second time, God's faithful preachers will have to bear a still more pointed testimony than was borne by John the Baptist. A responsible, important work is before them; and those who speak smooth things, God will not acknowledge as His shepherds. A fearful woe is upon them.

9T 22   The truth for this time is to appear in its power in the lives of those who believe it, and is to be imparted to the world.

9T 23 Regeneration is the only path by which we can enter the city of God. It is narrow, and the gate by which we enter is strait; but along it we are to lead men and women and children, teaching them that, in order to be saved, they must have a new heart and a new spirit. The old, hereditary traits of character must be overcome. The natural desires of the soul must be changed. All deception, all falsifying, all evil speaking, must be put away. The new life, which makes men and women Christlike is to be lived.

DA 353 Christ Himself did not suppress one word of truth, but He spoke it always in love. He exercised the greatest tact, and thoughtful, kind attention in His intercourse with the people. He was never rude, never needlessly spoke a severe word, never gave needless pain to a sensitive soul. He did not censure human weakness. He fearlessly denounced hypocrisy, unbelief, and iniquity, but tears were in His voice as He uttered His scathing rebukes. He wept over Jerusalem, the city He loved, that refused to receive Him, the Way, the Truth, and the Life. They rejected Him, the Saviour, but He regarded them with pitying tenderness, and sorrow so deep that it broke His heart. Every soul was precious in His eyes. While He always bore Himself with divine dignity, He bowed with tenderest regard to every member of the family of God. In all men He saw fallen souls whom it was His mission to save.

DA 356 Jesus Himself never purchased peace by compromise. His heart overflowed with love for the whole human race, but He was never indulgent to their sins. He was too much their friend to remain silent while they were pursuing a course that would ruin their souls.

RH January 7, 1890 When His doctrines were opposed, He defended them with so great zeal and certainty as to impress His hearers that He would die, if need be, to sustain the authority of His teachings.

RH October 29, 1901 Judging and reproving are two different things. God has laid upon His servants the work of reproving in love those who err; but He has forbidden and denounced the thoughtless judging so common among professed believers.

5T 147 Sin and sinners in the church must be promptly dealt with, that others may not be contaminated. Truth and purity require that we make more thorough work to cleanse the camp of Achans. Let those in responsible positions not suffer sin in a brother. Show him that he must either put away his sins or be separated from the church.

5T 482 Jesus was calm and gentle, not losing self-command, even when in stormy conflict, amid His fiercest elements of opposition.

COL 248 Sin is to be called by its right name, and is to be plainly laid out before the wrongdoer.

PP 578 Those who have too little courage to reprove wrong, or who through indolence or lack of interest make no earnest effort to purify the family or the church of God, are held accountable for the evil that may result from their neglect of duty. We are just as responsible for evils that we might have checked in others by exercise of parental or pastoral authority as if the acts had been our own.

Chapter 26
World Hates and Persecutes Righteousness

Matthew 5:10-13 Blessed are those who are persecuted for righteousness' sake, for theirs is the kingdom of heaven. Blessed are you when they revile and persecute you, and say all kinds of evil against you falsely for My sake. Rejoice and be exceedingly glad, for great is your reward in heaven, for so they persecuted the prophets who were before you.

Matthew 10:28 And do not fear those who kill the body but cannot kill the soul. But rather fear Him who is able to destroy both soul and body in hell.

Matthew 24:9-13 Then they will deliver you up to tribulation and kill you, and you will be hated by all nations for My name's sake. And then many will be offended, will betray one another, and will hate one another. Then many false prophets will rise up and deceive many. And because lawlessness will abound, the love of many will grow cold. But he who endures to the end shall be saved.

John 15:18-20, 16:2 If the world hates you, you know that it hated Me before it hated you. If you were of the world, the world would love its own. Yet because you are not of the world, but I chose you out of the world, therefore the world hates you. Remember the word that I said to you, "A servant is not greater than his master." If they persecuted Me, they will also persecute you…. They will put you out of the synagogues; yes, the time is coming that whoever kills you will think that he offers God service.

2 Timothy 3:12 All who desire to live godly in Christ Jesus will suffer persecution.

James 1:2-4 My brethren, count it all joy when you fall into various trials, knowing that the testing of your faith produces patience. But let patience have its perfect work, that you may be perfect and complete, lacking nothing.

James 4:4 Adulterers and adulteresses! Do you not know that friendship with the world is enmity with God? Whoever therefore wants to be a friend of the world makes himself an enemy of God.

1 Peter 2:20-23 For what credit is it if, when you are beaten for your faults, you take it patiently? But when you do good and suffer, if you take it patiently, this is commendable before God. For to this you were called, because Christ also suffered for us, leaving us an example, that you should follow His steps: "Who committed no sin, nor was deceit found in His mouth", who, when He was reviled, did not revile in return; when He suffered, He did not threaten, but committed Himself to Him who judges righteously.

1 Peter 3:14 But even if you should suffer for righteousness' sake, you are blessed. "And do not be afraid of their threats, nor be troubled."

1 Peter 4:12-13 Beloved, do not think it strange concerning the fiery trial which is to try you, as though some strange thing happened to you; but rejoice to the extent that you partake of Christ's sufferings, that when His glory is revealed, you may also be glad with exceeding joy.

1 Peter 4:16 Yet if anyone suffers as a Christian, let him not be ashamed, but let him glorify God in this matter.

1 John 3:12 Not as Cain who was of the wicked one and murdered his brother. And why did he murder him? Because his works were evil and his brother's righteous. Do not marvel, my brethren, if the world hates you.

MH 489 All our sufferings and sorrows, all our temptations and trials, all our sadness and griefs, all our persecutions and privations, in short, all things work together for our good. All experiences and circumstances are God's workmen whereby good is brought to us.

MB 71 The Father's presence encircled Christ, and nothing befell Him but that which infinite love permitted for the blessing of the world. Here was His source of comfort, and it is for us. He who is imbued with the Spirit of Christ abides in Christ. The blow that is aimed at him falls upon the Saviour, who surrounds him with His presence. Whatever comes to him comes from Christ. He has no need to resist evil, for Christ is his defense. Nothing can touch him except by our Lord's permission, and "all things" that are permitted "work together for good to them that love God." Romans 8:28.

Chapter 27
What to Do with Questions

Proverbs 3: 5-7 Trust in the LORD with all your heart, and lean not on your own understanding; In all your ways acknowledge Him, and He shall direct your paths. Do not be wise in your own eyes; fear the LORD and depart from evil.

Isaiah 55:6-9 Seek the LORD while He may be found, call upon Him while He is near. Let the wicked forsake his way, and the unrighteous man his thoughts; Let him return to the LORD, and He will have mercy on him; and to our God, for He will abundantly pardon. "For My thoughts are not your thoughts, nor are your ways My ways," says the Lord. "For as the heavens are higher than the earth, so are My ways higher than your ways, and My thoughts than your thoughts."

John 13:7 Jesus answered and said to him, "What I am doing you do not understand now, but you will know after this."

1 Corinthians 13:12 For now we see in a mirror, dimly, but then face to face. Now I know in part, but then I shall know just as I also am known.

SC 106 The entrance of sin into the world, the incarnation of Christ, regeneration, the resurrection, and many other subjects presented in the Bible are mysteries too deep for the human mind to explain, or even fully to comprehend. But we have no reason to doubt God's word because we cannot understand the mysteries of His providence.

SC 108 Because they cannot fathom all its mysteries, the skeptic and the infidel reject God's word; and not all who profess to believe the Bible are free from danger on this point…. A certain pride is mingled with the consideration of Bible truth, so that men feel impatient and defeated if they cannot explain every portion of Scripture to their satisfaction. It is too humiliating to them to acknowledge that they do not understand the inspired words. They are unwilling to wait patiently until God shall see fit to reveal the truth to them.

SC 109   If it were possible for created being to attain to a full understanding of God and His works, then, having reached this point, there would be for them no further discovery of truth, no growth in knowledge, no further development of mind and heart. God would no longer be supreme; and man, having reached the limit of knowledge and attainment, would cease to advance.... God intends that even in this life the truths of His word shall be ever unfolding to His people.

SC 110-111   Whenever men are not in word and deed seeking to be in harmony with God, then, however learned they may be, they are liable to err in their understanding of Scripture, and it is not safe to trust to their explanations. Those who look to Scriptures to find discrepancies, have not spiritual insight. With distorted vision they will see many causes for doubt and unbelief in things that are really plain and simple. Disguise it as they may, the real cause of doubt and skepticism, in most cases, is the love of sin. The teachings and restrictions of God's word are not welcome to the proud, sin-loving heart, and those who are unwilling to obey its requirements are ready to doubt its authority. In order to arrive at truth, we must have a sincere desire to know the truth and a willingness of heart to obey it. And all who come in this spirit to the study of the Bible will find abundant evidence that it is God's word, and they may gain an understanding of its truths that will make them wise unto salvation.

GC 528   There is but one course for those to pursue who honestly desire to be free from doubts. Instead of questioning and caviling concerning that which they do not understand, let them give heed to the light which already shines upon them, and they will receive greater light.

Chapter 28
I Don't Know a Perfect Christian

Genesis 6:9   Noah was a just man, perfect in his generations. Noah walked with God.

Daniel 6:21-22 Then Daniel said to the king, "O king, live forever! My God sent His angel and shut the lions' mouths, so that they have not hurt me, because I was found innocent before Him; and also, O king, I have done no wrong before you.

Luke 1:74-75 To grant us that we, being delivered from the hand of our enemies, might serve Him without fear, in holiness and righteousness before Him all the days of our life.

Colossians 1:21-23 And you, who once were alienated and enemies in your mind by wicked works, yet now He has reconciled in the body of His flesh through death, to present you holy, and blameless, and irreproachable in His sight – if indeed you continue in the faith, grounded and steadfast, and are not moved away from the hope of the gospel which you heard, which was preached to every creature under heaven.

1 Thessalonians 5:23   Now may the God of peace Himself sanctify you completely; and may your whole spirit, soul, and body be preserved blameless at the coming of our Lord Jesus Christ.

2 Timothy 4:7 I have fought the good fight, I have finished the race, I have kept the faith.

1 John 3:6 Whoever abides in Him does not sin.

Hebrews 11:4 By faith Abel offered unto God a more excellent sacrifice than Cain, by which he obtained witness that He was righteous.

Hebrews 11:7 By faith Noah, being divinely warned of things not yet seen, moved with godly fear, prepared an ark for the saving of his household; by the which he condemned the world, and became heir of the righteousness which is by faith.

SC 32   The impenitent sometimes excuse themselves by saying of professed Christians, "I am as good as they are." ....Thus they make the faults of others an excuse for their neglect of duty. But the sins and defects of others do not excuse anyone, for the Lord has not given us an erring human pattern. The spotless Son of God has been given as our example.

1SM 321   We may measures ourselves by ourselves, we may compare ourselves among ourselves, we may say we do as well as this one or that one, but the question to which the judgment will call for an answer is, Do we meet the claims of high heaven? Do we reach the divine standard? Are our hearts in harmony with the God of heaven?

AA 561   None of the apostles and prophets ever claimed to be without sin. Men who have lived the nearest to God, men who would sacrifice life itself rather than knowingly commit a wrong act, men whom God has honored with divine light and power, have confessed the sinfulness of their nature. They have put no confidence in the flesh, have claimed no righteousness of their own, but have trusted wholly in the righteousness of Christ.

1SP 378-379   Skeptics have assailed Christianity, and ridiculed the Bible, because David gave them occasion. They bring up to Christians the case of David, his sin in the case of Uriah and Bath-sheba, his polygamy, and then assert that David is called a man after God's own heart, and that if the Bible record is correct, God justified David in his crimes. I was shown that it was when David was pure, and walking in the counsel of God, that God called him a man after His own heart. When David departed from God, and stained his virtuous character by his crimes, he was no longer a man after God's own heart. God did not in the least degree justify his sins, but sent Nathan, His prophet, with dreadful denunciations to David because he had transgressed the commandment of the Lord. God shows his displeasure at David's having a plurality of wives by visiting him with judgments, and permitting evils to rise up against him from his own house. The terrible calamity that God permitted to come upon David; who, for his integrity, was once called a man after God's own heart, is evidence to after generations that God would not justify any one in transgressing His commandments; but that He would surely punish the guilty, however righteous and favored of God that they might once have been while they followed the Lord in purity of heart.

Chapter 29
Heathen Don't Have Excuse

Romans 1:18-20   For the wrath of God is revealed from heaven against all ungodliness and unrighteousness of men, who suppress the truth in unrighteousness, because what may be known of God is manifest in them, for God has shown it to them. For since the creation of the world His invisible attributes are clearly seen, being understood by the things that are made, even His eternal power and Godhead, so that they are without excuse.

Romans 2:13-16   (For not the hearers of the law are just in the sight of God, but the doers of the law will be justified; for when Gentiles, who do not have the law, by nature do the things in the law, these, although not having the law, are a law to themselves, who show the work of the law written in their hearts, their conscience also bearing witness, and between themselves their thoughts accusing or else excusing them) in the day when God will judge the secrets of men by Jesus Christ, according to my gospel.

DA 638   Those whom Christ commends in the judgement may have known little of theology, but they have cherished His principles. Through the influence of the divine Spirit they have been a blessing to those about them. Even among the heathen are those who have cherished the spirit of kindness; before the words of life had fallen upon their ears, they have befriended the missionaries, even ministering to them at the peril of their own lives. Among the heathen are those who worship God ignorantly, those to whom the light is never brought by human instrumentality, yet they will not perish. Though ignorant of the written law of God, they have heard His voice speaking to them in nature, and have done the things that the law required. Their works are evidence that the Holy Spirit has touched their hearts, and they are recognized as the children of God.

Chapter 30
The Big Picture

My study above involves dissecting the Bible passages and Ellen White quotes and categorizing them – so I could better understand each aspect of abiding in Christ. However, I believe it is important to look at the big picture – to then put all those parts together so they align. Each one is true by itself, but they are also true when put together. The more I read the Bible, the more I find it all points to the Gospel: Abiding in Christ. The following passages are areas where the big picture is seen:

**The Sanctuary Service Throughout Scripture
(especially Day of Atonement)
Matthew 5 - 7 Sermon on the Mount
Matthew 13 Parables Used to Describe Salvation
Matthew 25:1-13 Parable of the Wise and Foolish
Virgins
John 3:1-21 New Birth Conversation with Nicodemus
John 15:1-17 The True Vine
Acts 2:37-43 Disciples Convert 3,000
Romans 6 - 8
1 John**

Sanctuary

Outer Court: Justification (Being made right with God)
Enter His courts with praise – We enter God's presence
with praise and thankfulness for who He is
When an individual sinned they brought their lamb to be
sacrificed – Our individual sin killed Jesus. We need Jesus
as our personal Savior, for His blood to cleanse our sins
Sinner cut the fat out to be burned – we must separate sin
from our lives
Sacrifices were made morning and evening for
congregation – we are to worship God morning and
evening
Priest washed in laver – Christ cleanses us after we repent
of our sins

Holy Place: Living the Sanctified Life
Table of Showbread – we are to multiple times a day spend
time in God's Word
Candlestick – through the Holy Spirit, we are continually
receiving God's light and imparting it to the world
Altar of Incense – we are continually offering prayers to
God

Most Holy Place: Judgement of God
Ark of Covenant – God's law is His throne/character and
the covenant between us
Mercy Seat – The Lord gives mercy to those who confess
and forsake sins, even though we deserve death
Before Day of Atonement – 10 days spent searching life for
any hidden sin – we must be searching to eradicate all sin
Day of Atonement – 1 sin would cause death – when Christ
comes all sin must be confessed and eradicated

Matthew 25:1-13
Parable of the Wise and Foolish Virgins

10 Virgins – all with pure doctrine
Took their lamps – all reading the Bible
To meet the bridegroom – all preparing and looking for Jesus' return
5 wise – Whoever hears and does God's sayings Matthew 7:24
5 fools – Whoever hears and doesn't do God's sayings Matthew 7:26
Foolish took lamps with no oil – Had their Bible and some Holy Spirit
Wise took lamps and vessels with oil – Had their Bible and extra Holy Spirit in their vessels
While bridegroom delayed they all slept – We are ALL sleeping and not as awake as we should be as Jesus waits
Foolish didn't have enough oil to go into the wedding – Had partially followed Holy Spirit, but not completely
How do we get more oil? We lose oil (Holy Spirit) by not obeying when He speaks; we gain oil by obeying Holy Spirit when He speaks
Foolish virgins returned and cried to open door. Jesus said, "I do not know you." There wasn't an abiding relationship.

COL 411 The class represented by the foolish virgins are not hypocrites. They have a regard for the truth, they have advocated the truth, they are attracted to those who believe the truth; but they have not yielded themselves to the Holy Spirit's working. They have not fallen upon the Rock, Christ Jesus, and permitted their old nature to be broken up.... The Spirit works upon man's heart, according to his desire and consent implanting in him a new nature; but the class represented by the foolish virgins have been content with a superficial work. They do not know God.

John 15

Jesus the True Vine

15 [1]"I am the true vine, and My Father is the vinedresser. [2] Every branch in Me that does not bear fruit He takes away; and every branch that bears fruit He prunes, that it may bear more fruit. [3] You are already clean because of the word which I have spoken to you. [4] Abide in Me, and I in you. As the branch cannot bear fruit of itself, unless it abides in the vine, neither can you, unless you abide in Me. [5] I am the vine, you are the branches. He who abides in Me, and I in him, bears much fruit; for without Me you can do nothing. [6] If anyone does not abide in Me, he is cast out as a branch and is withered; and they gather them and throw them into the fire, and they are burned. [7] If you abide in Me, and My words abide in you, you will ask what you desire, and it shall be done for you. [8] By this My Father is glorified, that you bear much fruit; so you will be My disciples.

[9] "As the Father loved Me, I also have loved you; abide in My love. [10] If you keep My commandments, you will abide in My love, just as I have kept My Father's commandments and abide in His love. [11] These things I have spoken to you, that My joy may remain in you, and that your joy may be full. [12] This is My commandment, that you love one another as I have loved you. [13] Greater love has no one than this, than to lay down one's life for his friends. [14] You are My friends if you do whatever I command you. [15] No longer do I call you servants, for a servant does not know what his master is doing; but I have called you friends, for all things that I heard from My Father I have made known to you. [16] You did not choose Me, but I chose you and appointed you that you should go and bear fruit, and that your fruit should remain, that whatever you ask the Father in My name He may give you. [17] These things I command you, that you love one another."

The World's Hatred

[18] "If the world hates you, you know that it hated Me before it hated you. [19] If you were of the world, the world would love its own. Yet because you are not of the world, but I chose you out of the world, therefore the world hates you. [20] Remember the word that I said to you, 'A servant is not greater than his master.' If they persecuted Me, they will also persecute you. If they kept My word, they will keep yours also. [21] But all these things they will do to you for My name's sake, because they do not know Him who sent Me. [22] If I had not come and spoken to them, they would have no sin, but now they have no excuse for their sin. [23] He who hates Me hates My Father also. [24] If I had not done among them the works which no one else did, they would have no sin; but now they have seen and also hated both Me and My Father. [25] But this happened that the word might be fulfilled which is written in their law, 'They hated Me without a cause.'"

[26] "But when the Helper comes, whom I shall send to you from the Father, the Spirit of truth who proceeds from the Father, He will testify of Me. [27] And you also will bear witness, because you have been with Me from the beginning."

Romans 6-8

Dead to Sin but Alive in Christ

6 [1]"What shall we say then? Shall we continue in sin that grace may abound? [2] Certainly not! How shall we who died to sin live any longer in it? [3] Or do you not know that as many of us as were baptized into Christ Jesus were baptized into His death? [4] Therefore we were buried with Him through baptism into death, that just as Christ was raised from the dead by the glory of the Father, even so we also should walk in newness of life. [5] For if we have been united together in the likeness of His death, certainly we also shall be in the likeness of His resurrection, [6] knowing this, that our old man was crucified with Him, that the body of sin might be done away with, that we should no longer be slaves of sin. [7] For he who has died has been freed from sin. [8] Now if we died with Christ, we believe that we shall also live with Him, [9] knowing that Christ, having been raised from the dead, dies no more. Death no longer has dominion over Him. [10] For the death that He died, He died to sin once for all; but the life that He lives, He lives to God. [11] Likewise you also, reckon yourselves to be dead indeed to sin, but alive to God in Christ Jesus our Lord."

[12]"Therefore do not let sin reign in your mortal body, that you should obey it in its lusts. [13] And do not present your members as instruments of unrighteousness to sin, but present yourselves to God as being alive from the dead, and your members as instruments of righteousness to God. [14]For sin shall not have dominion over you, for you are not under law but under grace."

Servants of Righteousness

[15]"What then? Shall we sin because we are not under law but under grace? Certainly not! [16] Do you not know that to whom you present yourselves slaves to obey, you are that one's slaves whom you obey, whether of sin leading to death,

or of obedience leading to righteousness? [17] But God be thanked that though you were slaves of sin, yet you obeyed from the heart that form of doctrine to which you were delivered. [18] And having been set free from sin, you became slaves of righteousness. [19] I speak in human terms because of the weakness of your flesh. For just as you presented your members as slaves of uncleanness, and of lawlessness leading to more lawlessness, so now present your members as slaves of righteousness for holiness. [20] For when you were slaves of sin, you were free in regard to righteousness. [21] What fruit did you have then in the things of which you are now ashamed? For the end of those things is death. [22] But now having been set free from sin, and having become slaves of God, you have your fruit to holiness, and the end, everlasting life. [23] For the wages of sin is death, but the gift of God is eternal life in Christ Jesus our Lord."

An Analogy from Marriage

7 [1]"Or do you not know, brethren (for I speak to those who know the law), that the law has dominion over a man as long as he lives? [2] For the woman who has a husband is bound by the law to her husband as long as he lives. But if the husband dies, she is released from the law of her husband. [3] So then if, while her husband lives, she marries another man, she will be called an adulteress; but if her husband dies, she is free from that law, so that she is no adulteress, though she has married another man. [4] Therefore, my brethren, you also have become dead to the law through the body of Christ, that you may be married to another – to Him who was raised from the dead, that we should bear fruit to God. [5] For when we were in the flesh, the sinful passions which were aroused by the law were at work in our members to bear fruit to death. [6] But now we have been delivered from the law, having died to what we were held by, so that we

should serve in the newness of the Spirit and not in the oldness of the letter."

The Problem of Indwelling Sin

[7]"What shall we say then? Is the law sin? Certainly not! On the contrary, I would not have known sin except through the law. For I would not have known covetousness unless the law had said, "You shall not covet." [8] But sin, taking opportunity by the commandment, produced in me all manner of evil desire. For apart from the law sin was dead. [9] I was alive once without the law, but when the commandment came, sin revived and I died. [10] And the commandment, which was to bring life, I found to bring death. [11] For sin, taking occasion by the commandment, deceived me, and by it killed me. [12] Therefore the law is holy, and the commandment holy and just and good. [13] Has then what is good become death to me? Certainly not! But sin, that it might appear sin, was producing death in me through what is good, so that sin through the commandment might become exceedingly sinful."

[14]"For we know that the law is spiritual, but I am carnal, sold under sin. [15] For what I am doing, I do not understand. For what I will to do, that I do not practice; but what I hate, that I do. [16] If, then, I do what I will not to do, I agree with the law that it is good. [17] But now, it is no longer I who do it, but sin that dwells in me. [18] For I know that in me (that is, in my flesh) nothing good dwells; for to will is present with me, but how to perform what is good I do not find. [19] For the good that I will to do, I do not do; but the evil I will not to do, that I practice. [20] Now if I do what I will not to do, it is no longer I who do it, but sin that dwells in me. [21] I find then a law, that evil is present with me, the one who wills to do good. [22] For I delight in the law of God according to the inward man. [23] But I see another law in my members, warring against the law of my mind, and bringing me into captivity to the law of sin which is in my members. [24] O

wretched man that I am! Who will deliver me from this body of death? 25 I thank God – through Jesus Christ our Lord! So then, with the mind I myself serve the law of God, but with the flesh the law of sin."

Life in the Spirit

8 1"There is therefore now no condemnation to those who are in Christ Jesus, who do not walk according to the flesh, but according to the Spirit. 2 For the law of the Spirit of life in Christ Jesus has made me free from the law of sin and death. 3 For what the law could not do in that it was weak through the flesh, God did by sending His own Son in the likeness of sinful flesh, on account of sin: He condemned sin in the flesh, 4 that the righteous requirement of the law might be fulfilled in us who do not walk according to the flesh but according to the Spirit. 5 For those who live according to the flesh set their minds on the things of the flesh, but those who live according to the Spirit, the things of the Spirit. 6 For to be carnally minded is death, but to be spiritually minded is life and peace. 7 Because the carnal mind is enmity against God; for it is not subject to the law of God, nor indeed can be. 8 So then, those who are in the flesh cannot please God. 9 But you are not in the flesh but in the Spirit, if indeed the Spirit of God dwells in you. Now if anyone does not have the Spirit of Christ, he is not His."

10"And if Christ is in you, the body is dead because of sin, but the Spirit is life because of righteousness. 11 But if the Spirit of Him who raised Jesus from the dead dwells in you, He who raised Christ from the dead will also give life to your mortal bodies through His Spirit who dwells in you. 12 Therefore, brethren, we are debtors – not to the flesh, to live according to the flesh. 13 For if you live according to the flesh you will die; but if by the Spirit you put to death the deeds of the body, you will live. 14 For as many as are led by the Spirit of God, these are sons of God. 15 For you did not receive the spirit of bondage again to fear, but you received the Spirit of adoption by whom we cry out, "Abba, Father." [16] The Spirit Himself bears witness with our spirit that we are children of God, [17] and if children, then heirs - heirs of God and joint heirs with Christ, if indeed we suffer with Him, that we may also be glorified together. [18] For I consider that the sufferings of this present time are not worthy to be compared with the glory which shall be revealed in us. [19] For the earnest expectation of the creation eagerly waits for the revealing of the sons of God. [20] For the creation was subjected to futility, not willingly, but because of Him who subjected it in hope; [21] because the creation itself also will be delivered from the bondage of corruption into the glorious liberty of the children of God. [22] For we know that the whole creation groans and labors with birth pangs together until now. [23] Not only that, but we also who have the firstfruits of the Spirit, even we ourselves groan within ourselves, eagerly waiting for the adoption, the redemption of our body. [24] For we were saved in this hope, but hope that is seen is not hope; for why does one still hope for what he sees? [25] But if we hope for what we do not see, we eagerly wait for it with perseverance."

[26]"Likewise the Spirit also helps in our weaknesses. For we do not know what we should pray for as we ought, but the Spirit Himself makes intercession for us with groanings which cannot be uttered. [27] Now He who searches the hearts knows what the mind of the Spirit is, because He makes intercession for the saints according to the will of God."

More than Conquerors

[28]"And we know that all things work together for good to those who love God, to those who are the called according to His purpose. [29] For whom He foreknew, He also predestined to be conformed to the image of His Son, that He might be the firstborn among many brethren. [30]Moreover whom He predestined, these He also called; whom He called, these He also justified; and whom He justified, these

He also glorified. [31] What then shall we say to these things? If God is for us, who can be against us? [32] He who did not spare His own Son, but delivered Him up for us all, how shall He not with Him also freely give us all things? [33] Who shall bring a charge against God's elect? It is God who justifies. [34] Who is he who condemns? It is Christ who died, and furthermore is also risen, who is even at the right hand of God, who also makes intercession for us. [35] Who shall separate us from the love of Christ? Shall tribulation, or distress, or persecution, or famine, or nakedness, or peril, or sword? [36] As it is written: "For Your sake we are killed all day long; We are accounted as sheep for the slaughter." [37] Yet in all these things we are more than conquerors through Him who loved us. [38] For I am persuaded that neither death nor life, nor angels nor principalities nor powers, nor things present nor things to come, [39] nor height nor depth, nor any other created thing, shall be able to separate us from the love of God which is in Christ Jesus our Lord."

Chapter 31
Conclusion

Sin is the most dangerous thing on planet Earth. It kills everyone it is in. As God is love, Satan is sin. We were all unfortunately through our unfaithful father Adam, born with a sinful nature. Every act of our sin is allegiance to Satan and is further reproducing his character within us. To "Christians," Satan has very cunningly taught us it is ok to believe in the law, but just realize it isn't possible to obey. By doing this, we are deceived: believing we are saved, when our hearts and works testify we are lost. Our hearts and works testify whose nature we have – who we follow. God kicked sin out of heaven and Eden the first time, and He won't let it back in a second time. This all sounds terrible and you may wonder why I even say this. Because we have avoided this. We haven't stopped to see our terrible condition. And that is why we haven't become converted; we haven't changed. We haven't seen our need for a Saviour, and so we haven't searched for a Saviour. To be converted, we must realize the truth of who we are and our need of a Saviour.

But there is excellent news: Christ came to this world to take away sin – that IS the gospel! He came to save a wretch like me! God offers to live inside of me and live His victory through me TODAY! When He is abiding in my heart, I am His holy temple. When He is in my heart, I cannot sin – for He cannot sin. He becomes the power of victory in my life to both rescue me and keep me from sin! And he has prepared Heaven in which there is no sin, sorrow, or heartache. It is a promise – for eternity! If I allow Him to live in me and create a new heart and mind in me, I will live a meaningful and powerful life here on Earth. And when He comes back to take His children home, I will go to live in that heavenly country with Him face to face!

The way to come to Christ is the simplest method, and yet the hardest. Simple because we just have to give up. Hard because we must be willing to give up and surrender moment by moment to Christ. It begins with true repentance: seeing how awful we are, repenting, and choosing to die to self and let Christ live within us. This isn't a once in a lifetime conversion – this is a daily consecration through reading His Word, talking to Him, and committing to trustingly listen and obey His voice. If we step away from Him and sin – we must acknowledge it as sin that separates us from Christ and grows us into the image of Satan - but we can repent while there is time! – for we have a Mediator!

Christ is Righteousness. Christ is Love. Everything in and of myself is evil. I cannot produce one act of righteousness or love. I need to abide in Christ. I need Christ to take control of my heart and mind and change it. But He does that only if I will Him to – each moment of the day. Satan will dangle before me crafty lies, distractions, and the thought of self to try and get me off track. The Holy Spirit will guide me, and if I listen and obey – I will experience victory after victory. That is sanctification: moment by moment abiding and living out His righteousness.

While abiding in Christ I will always be growing. It is as a school teacher who prepares her students for one level at a time. They love to listen and learn. At each level they are given a test and pass with 100%. They are then moved onto the next level of knowledge. And it continues for all time. The other growing that needs to occur is that in my sinful flesh, I have neural pathways that have been formed in sin. This has produced my character of sin. When I first come to Jesus, it is difficult (but possible) for me to put to death the flesh and surrender my will to Christ in obedience. Each time I obey, I am slowly putting to death the previous neural pathway and forming a new neural pathway of righteousness. The more I do this, the more it is my desire

164

and habit to obey. Adam before sin, and Christ who lived sinlessly, needed to form a righteous character through obedience. We must also form righteous characters from obedience so we will not ever want to sin again.

Christ is waiting for His harvest to ripen so He can come to Earth and take His children home. Today is the day of salvation. Today I choose to reject the crafty lies and believe the powerful truth of the gospel – of Jesus Christ Himself. Today I choose to let Him move in and cleanse my temple – to kick the devil out. Today, and moment by moment, I choose to humbly submit to Jesus. I desire to grow in Him more and more each day, and fall greater in love with Him for all eternity.

Chapter 32
Further Study

Bible in its entirety

Steps to Christ by Ellen White

Christ's Object Lessons by Ellen White

What Shall I Do To Inherit Eternal Life by Margaret Davis
www.whatshallido.org

The Life of Victory by Meade Macguire
(Reprinted copies available at truthinjesuspublications@gmail.com)

Guide to Christian Perfection by Charles Fitch
(Available at www.TEACHServices.com)

Lessons on Faith by Alonzo T. Jones & Ellet J. Waggoner
(Available at www.TEACHServices.com)

His Robe or Mine by Frank Phillips
Branch and the Vine by Frank Phillips
www.JustifiedWalk.com

Christ Our Righteousness by J.W. "Bill" Lehman

Everlasting Covenant by E. J. Waggoner

www.Eternalrealities.com

Further Information on our Family and Ministry

www.NewHearts4Christ.com
www.Victoryfromallsin.com

Key to Abbreviations of Ellen White Book Titles

AA	Acts of the Apostles
AH	Adventist Home
CG	Child Guidance
CCh	Counsels for the Church
CD	Counsels on Diet and Foods
COL	Christ's Object Lessons
CT	Counsels to Teachers
DA	The Desire of Ages
ED	Education
EW	Early Writings
FLB	The Faith I Live By
FW	Faith and Works
GC	Great Controversy
GW	Gospel Workers
HP	In Heavenly Places
MB	Mount of Blessing
MH	Ministry of Healing
ML	My Life Today
MS	Manuscript
MYP	Messages to Young People
OHC	Our High Calling
PK	Prophets and Kings
PP	Patriarchs and Prophets
RH	Review and Herald
SC	Steps to Christ
SD	Sons and Daughters
SM	Selected Messages
SP	Spirit of Prophecy
ST	Signs of the Times
T	Testimonies for the Church Volumes 1-9
Te	Temperance
TDG	This Day With God
TM	Testimonies to Ministers
TMK	That I May Know Him